yorkshire shores

the traditional fisherman's sweater, known as a gansey, has been knitted in Yorkshire for almost 200 years. Distinctive due to the combination of small knit and purl patterns with cables, the gansey was a seaman's everyday wear (and often his Sunday best too).

Yorkshire Shores takes inspiration from the stitch patterns used in traditional Yorkshire ganseys, with knits for everyone to create, wear and use every day. Similarly to original sweaters, the nine designs in this book are constructed with minimal sewing required: garment bodies are made in one piece, sleeve stitches are picked up and knitted down, and shoulder seams are joined with 3-needle cast offs.

All of the designs featured are knitted in baa ram ewe Dovestone DK, a blend of Masham, Wensleydale and Bluefaced Leicester: 100% British wool, spun and dyed in Yorkshire. Its softly heathered shades and springy woolliness result in beautiful, warm and cosy knits: a year-round requirement for the British seaside!

baa ram ewe

contents

ganseys

a gansey is a traditional hand-knitted jumper worn by fishermen, particularly herring fishers, down the coast of Britain. These practical garments have been made for almost two centuries, originally using simple patterns but as time passed the stitches became more varied and complex. Ganseys offered protection for workers from the elements when at sea but were also versatile enough to wear year-round on shore too.

WHAT MAKES A GANSEY?

To achieve the desired tight knit, ganseys are traditionally worked in one piece on five thin steel DPNs using closely spun 5 ply worsted wool, sometimes known as "Seaman's iron". This construction provides strength and forms a single protective shell around the wearer, with an underarm diamond shaped gusset and sometimes split welt allowing for movement. Worked from the bottom up, the body is worked as a tube to the armpit gusset, then the stitches are halved and worked flat to the shoulders. These are then joined together in a three-needle cast off leaving space for the neckband at the centre, which is then picked up and worked to desired length. The arms are picked up at the edge of the side and knit to the required length finishing with tight ribbing at the cuff.

The patterning, which can be all over or just at the yoke, is identical front and back, with some styles extending motifs down the tops of the arms providing an extra layer of protection from poor weather conditions. This reflection of motifs means ganseys are reversible, evening out the wear at vulnerable points such as the elbows. The lower sleeves were mostly knit plain, allowing them to be easily pulled back and reknit if damaged by knives or hooks at sea. A lack of seams and good dense material means these garments are practical in design and, most importantly, splash and windproof.

It is often said that gansey patterns could be used to identify dead sailors who were washed ashore, by the association of particular stitch patterns with villages. Although this may have been true for the early garments, as time passed the patterns became less defined in each village and fishermen would travel to the best fishing grounds to earn a living without changing their ganseys.

It has been questioned whether J.M. Synge's play *Riders to the Sea* (1904) is the inspiration for this folklore. In the play a sailor's body is identified by his knitted jumper, however, there is no mention that stitch patterns are associated with his home village, merely that the knitter recognises their own handiwork. There are arguments both for and against the i.d. tag-style use of motifs as a legitimate reason for such varied gansey patterns; perhaps a conclusion will never be reached.

Another principle that has been observed in the book is the omission of the use of green yarns in a gansey pattern. This is because in parts of Yorkshire, particularly in (although not limited to) the Humber area, it is perceived as an unlucky colour when associated with the sea.

Some tales say it is the colour of Davy Jones' locker, while others say the connection of the colour to land is too strong. Boats painted in the colour are said to wander back to port without a sailor's bidding, while wearing green is considered a bad omen – sailors are known to be superstitious! Therefore, rather than tempt fate, our Chevin and Dalby shades have been kept well away from the *Yorkshire Shores* collection.

special techniques

3-NEEDLE CAST OFF

Hold both needles in your left hand with right sides together and wrong side facing.

With a third needle, knit 1 stitch from the front needle and 1 stitch from the back needle together. *Knit the next stitch from the front needle together with the next stitch from the back needle, then lift the first stitch on the right needle over the second one; rep from * until all stitches have been cast off.

GRAFTING (KITCHENER STITCH)

Ensuring stitches are evenly distributed on two needles, hold both needles in your left hand with right side facing.

Using a tapestry needle and a length of yarn three times the length of the piece to be grafted, bring the needle through the first stitch on the front needle purlwise, leaving the stitch on the needle, then bring the needle through the first stitch on the back needle knitwise, leaving the stitch on the needle.

1. Bring the needle through the first stitch on the front needle knitwise and slip it off the needle,
2. then through the second stitch on the front needle purlwise, leaving it on the needle,
3. then through the first stitch on the back needle purlwise and slip it off the needle,
4. then through the second stitch on the back needle knitwise, leaving it on the needle.
5. Rep steps 1-4 until all stitches have been worked. For the last stitch on each needle, work step 1 followed by step 3.
6. Finally, adjust the tension of the grafting to match the tension of the knitting.

WRAP & TURN

After a knit stitch

Bring the yarn to the front between the needles. Slip the next stitch purlwise. Take the yarn to the back between the needles. Slip stitch back to left needle. Turn.

After a purl stitch

Bring the yarn to the back between the needles. Slip the next stitch purlwise. Take the yarn to the front between the needles. Slip stitch back to left needle. Turn.

To pick up a wrap on a knit stitch

Use right needle to pick up the wrap from the front to the back, then put needle into the stitch knitwise, knit wrap and stitch together.

To pick up a wrap on a purl stitch

Use the right needle to pick up the wrap from the back to the front and place it on the left needle. Purl the wrap and the stitch together.

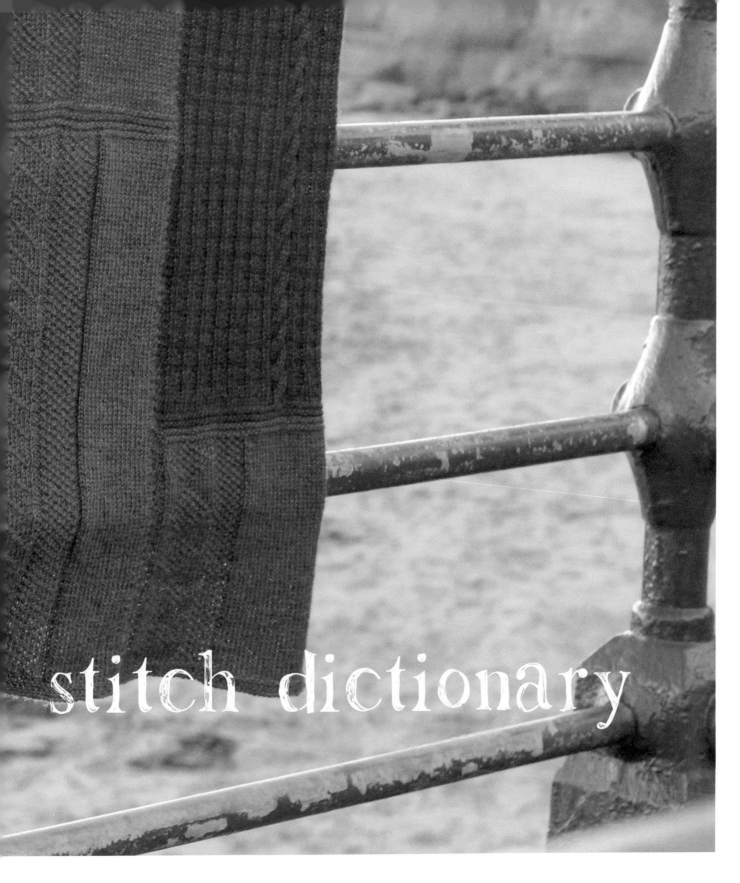

stitch dictionary

stitch dictionary

The origins and meanings of the most commonly used gansey stitch patterns.

CABLES OR ROPES

Cables, sometimes known as 'links of love', are common across many ganseys and can be used as part of the main design or simply to break up large areas of pattern. Probably the easiest stitch combination to recognise, the simplest interpretation of these is the ropes used aboard the fishing ships for a myriad of roles. A more conceptual view is that it shows the hard work that holds together a family or community, due to fishing being the main source of income when these patterns were first knit.

Practically, cables trap huge amounts of air within the cross-over making the garment very insulating. The doubling of fabric also helped cushion the chest. The twist is traditionally worked a row after the expected line (nth+1) row, for example a 4 st cable would twist every 5th row.

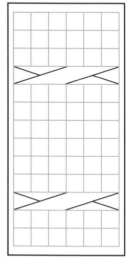

HERRINGBONE

Herringbone is a pictographic motif, it shows the fish being caught by the men at sea and sorted by the women on shore. These fish were the main staple income for many travelling up and down the coast following the shoals to make a living. Many wives of fishermen, who would knit the ganseys, were known as "herring girls".

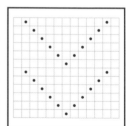

BETTY MARTIN

A simple but effective pattern, Betty Martin can be found worked in small areas of a pattern up to whole swathes. Though the origin of the name is not strictly known, it is sometimes attributed to the local Whitby knitter by the same name who taught many locals and new-comers gansey lore and construction. It would seem she was known as a bit of a local celebrity, thus giving her signature stitch its name. It is best associated with variations of the Whitby & Filey patterns.

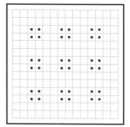

NET MASK OR DIAMONDS

Easily identifiable, the meaning of the Net Mask stitch is almost impossible to argue. It is a fisherman's most valued tool, his nets, sometimes shown with or without a moss stitch filling. Quick and intuitive to knit, this motif often repeats the full length of a gansey. Locations that traditionally use this pattern are mostly found around the Hull area, such as the Humberside Keel, Bridlington and Flamborough ganseys.

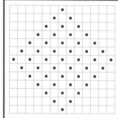

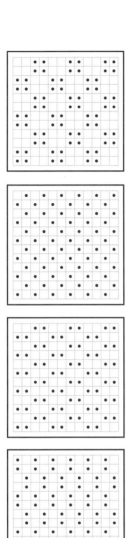

BASKET

A simple combination of 2x2 knit and purl squares are used to raise small areas of fabric, trapping more air and helping with to keep the wearer warm and protected from the elements. This stitch illustrates the baskets that held the daily catch as it came ashore and was sold in the market. Simple and effective, it needs very little concentration to knit, making it perfect as a filler or type of seed stitch.

MOSS OR SEED

A common seeding stitch, Moss is sometimes known as 'sand and shingle' or 'Cat's een'. It is often used as filler on ganseys, as it is simple to follow but adds plenty of texture to a surface, trapping air and warmth. There are variations on this stitch ranging from the common 1x1 knit and purl to uneven combinations of 2x1, both vertically and horizontally.

MOSS OR SEED

1 x 2 horizontal Moss

MOSS OR SEED

2 x 1 vertical Moss

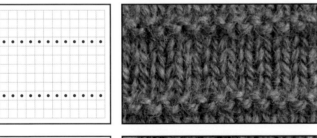

LADDERS OR STEPS

Most recognisably found at the edge of the Scarborough pattern, ladders or steps have several meanings. When referred to as the 'Ladder to God' this simple pattern means the local village has a church or the wearer has a close association with the clergy. Visually the raised purl rows act as the rungs on a ladder from a pier down to a docked boat. Metaphorically, the steps are stages to success, i.e. a man who has done well or strives hard for his family, though this is a lesser-known interpretation.

Commonly found as single purl ridges separated by 4 rows of stocking stitch, this stitch can be knit in a variety of combinations. Neither the distance between the rungs or the thickness of each ridge is set. Here we have shown two possible variations; the usual four rows St st with 1 purl row (above) and an equally balanced two rows of each option (left).

baa ram ewe YORKSHIRE SHORES

yorkshire shores
PATTERNS

ravenscar hat

by Graeme Knowles-Miller

Inspired by the headland between Robin Hood's Bay and Scarborough, this hat combines samples of motifs found in ganseys along the Yorkshire coast. With all sizes using one skein, this quick and easy project is perfect for practising gansey stitches.

YARN USED
baa ram ewe Dovestone DK in shade:
Lotherton, 1 (1, 1) x 100g skein

GAUGE
22 sts x 30 rows = 10cm/4" blocked and measured over stocking stitch on 4mm (US 6) needles

NEEDLES USED
3.5mm (US 4) circular needle, 40cm/16" length
4mm (US 6) circular needle, 40cm/16" length
4mm (US 6) DPNs for shaping the crown

OTHER SUPPLIES
6 stitch markers
Cable needle

SIZING
Sizes: 1 (2, 3)
To fit head size: 46 (51, 56)cm/18 (20, 22)" worn with 1.25cm/½" negative ease

ABBREVIATIONS
A list of standard abbreviations appears on page 72 and also on both cover flaps.

SPECIAL INSTRUCTIONS
CABLE
C4B: Slip 2 sts to cn and hold in back, k2, k2 from cn.

WRITTEN INSTRUCTIONS

RIB
Using 3.5mm ndl, cast on 96 (108, 120) sts. Join to work in the rnd, being careful not to twist and pm to indicate beg of rnd.

Rnd 1: *K1, p1; rep from * to end.
Rep rnd 1 until work measures 3cm/1¼" from cast-on edge.

BODY
Change to 4mm ndl.
Rnds 1-2: Knit.
Rnds 3-4: Purl.
Rnds 5-8: Rep rnds 1-4.
Rnd 9: Knit.
Rnds 10-11: *K1, p1; rep from * to end.
Rnds 12-13: *P1, k1; rep from * to end.
Rnds 14-17: Rep rnds 10-13.
Rnd 18: Knit.
Rnds 19-20: Purl.
Rnds 21-22: Knit.
Rnds 23-25: Rep rnds 19-21.
Rnd 26: *P1, k4, p1, k1, p2, k1, p6 (6, 7), k0 (1, 3); rep from * a further 5 times.
Rnd 27: *P1, k4, p1, k1, p2, k1, p5, k1, p0 (2, 4); rep from * a further 5 times.
Rnd 28: *[P1, k4] twice, p4, k2, p0 (1, 1), k0 (1, 3); rep from * a further 5 times.

Rnd 29: *[P1, k4] twice, p3, k3, p0 (2, 4); rep from * a further 5 times.

Rnd 30: *P1, C4B, p1, k1, p2, k1, p2, k4, p0 (1, 1), k0 (1, 3); rep from * a further 5 times.

Rnd 31: *P1, k4, p1, k1, p2, k1, p1, k5, p0 (2, 4); rep from * a further 5 times.

Rnd 32: *[P1, k4] twice, p6 (7, 7), k0 (1, 3); rep from * a further 5 times.

Rnd 33: *P1, k4, p1, k1, p2, k1, p5, k1, p0 (2, 4); rep from * a further 5 times.

Rnd 34: *P1, k4, p1, k1, p2, k1, p4, k2, p0 (1, 1), k0 (1, 3); rep from * a further 5 times.

Rnd 35: *P1, C4B, p1, k1, p2, k1, p3, k3, p0 (2, 4); rep from * a further 5 times.

Rnd 36: *[P1, k4] twice, p2, k4, p0 (1, 1), k0 (1, 3); rep from * a further 5 times.

Rnd 37: *[P1, k4] twice, p1, k5, p0 (2, 4); rep from * a further 5 times.

Rnd 38: Rep rnd 26.

Rnd 39: Rep rnd 27.

Rnd 40: *P1, C4B, p1, k4, p4, k2, p0 (1, 1), k0 (1, 3); rep from * a further 5 times.

Rnd 41: Rep rnd 29.

Rnd 42: Rep rnd 36.

Rnd 43: Rep rnd 37.

Rnd 44: Rep rnd 38.

Rnd 45: Knit.

Rnds 46-47: Purl.

Rnd 48: Knit.

Rnd 49: *K16 (18, 20), pm; rep from * a further 5 times noting that the sixth marker will be the beg of rnd marker already in place.

CROWN

Shape the crown as follows, changing to DPNs as the stitch count decreases.

Rnd 50: *P2tog, ssp, p to m, sm; rep from * a further 5 times. *84 (96, 108) sts*

Rnd 51: Purl.

Rnd 52: *K2, p2; rep from * to end.

SIZES 1 & 3 ONLY

Rnd 53: *P2tog, ssp, p2, [k2, p2] to m, sm; rep from * a further 5 times. *72 (-, 96) sts*

SIZE 2 ONLY
Rnd 53: *P2tog, ssp, [p2, k2] to m, sm; rep from * a further 5 times. *84 sts*

ALL SIZES AGAIN
Rnds 54-55: Purl.
Rnd 56: *K2tog, ssk, k to m, sm; rep from * a further 5 times. *60 (72, 84) sts*
Rnd 57: Knit.
Rnd 58: Purl.
Rnd 59: *P2tog, ssp, p to m, sm; rep from * a further 5 times. *48 (60, 72) sts*
Rnds 60-61: *K2, p2; rep from * to end.
Rnd 62: *P2tog, ssp, p to m, sm; rep from * a further 5 times. *36 (48, 60) sts*
Rnd 63: Purl.
Rnd 64: Knit.
Rnd 65: *K2tog, ssk, k to m, sm; rep from * a further 5 times. *24 (36, 48) sts*
Rnds 66-67: Purl.
Rnd 68: *P2tog, ssp, k0 (2, 2), p0 (0, 2), sm; rep from * a further 5 times. *12 (24, 36) sts*

SIZE 2 ONLY
Rnd 69: *P2, k2, sm; rep from * a further 5 times.
Rnd 70: Purl.
Rnd 71: *K2tog, ssk; rep from * a further 5 times.

SIZE 3 ONLY
Rnd 69: *P2, k2, rm; rep from * a further 5 times but leaving beg of rnd marker in place.
Rnd 70: Purl.
Rnd 71: *P2tog, ssp, p2; rep from * a further 5 times. *24 sts*
Rnd 72: Knit
Rnd 73: Knit
Rnd 74: *K2tog, ssk; rep from * a further 5 times. *12 sts*

ALL SIZES AGAIN
Next rnd: [K2tog] to end. *6 sts*
Break yarn leaving a 15cm/6" tail. Thread the tail through the live sts and gather before securing on the inside of the hat.

FINISHING
Weave in ends and block to measurements taking care not to overstretch the rib.

filey

by Alison Moreton

Inspired by "Filey Pattern X" in *Patterns for Guernseys, Jerseys and Arans*, these mitts use side-to-side construction with a 3-needle cast off, afterthought thumb and cuff placket for a quick project with lots of interesting details.

PATTERN NOTES
Perhaps a little unusually, in the original pattern the cable was crossed every 6th row, just as in the pattern here (this is in contrast to many of the patterns recorded where a six stitch cable was crossed every 7th row).

YARN USED
baa ram ewe Dovestone DK in shade:
Filey, 1 x 100g skein

GAUGE
26 sts x 34 rows = 10cm/4" blocked and measured over stocking stitch on 3.75mm (US 6) needles

NEEDLES USED
3.75mm (US 5) knitting needles
3.75mm (US 5) DPNs

OTHER SUPPLIES
Cable needle
Locking stitch marker
Stitch marker
Smooth DK weight scrap yarn
6 buttons, 9mm/⅓" diameter

SIZING
One size
18cm/7" circumference
21cm/8¼" length
To fit women's medium hand worn with 1.25cm/½" negative ease or up to 1.25cm/½" positive ease – see Hints & Tips below for details on how to adjust the size.

ABBREVIATIONS
A list of standard abbreviations appears on page 72 and also on both cover flaps.

SPECIAL INSTRUCTIONS
CABLE
C6B: Slip 3 sts to cn and hold in back, k3, k3 from cn.

HINTS AND TIPS
To adjust for a larger or smaller hand, work the section up to placing the afterthought thumb to a longer or shorter length (half the desired finished circumference). Work the same length after placing the thumb.
To adjust the afterthought thumb, use a needle one size larger or smaller when working the thumb for a slightly looser or tighter fit

WRITTEN INSTRUCTIONS

LEFT MITT
Using 3.75mm ndls, cast on 51 sts.

Row 1 (RS): K13, place a locking stitch marker in last st worked, k to end.
Row 2 (WS) (Buttonholes): K to last 12 sts, *k2tog, yo, k2; rep from * to end. *3 buttonholes made*

**
Rows 3-4: Knit.
Row 5: K2, p2, m1, k4, m1, p2, [k1, p1] 3 times, k1, p2, k6, p1, k6, p2, [k1, p1] 3 times, k1, p2, m1, k4, m1, p2, k2. *55 sts*

COMMENCE MAIN PATTERN:
Reading from the Chart or Written Instructions, starting with WS row 1, rep patt rows 1-6 until piece measures 9cm/3½" from cast-on edge ending with a WS row.
***

CHART - WRITTEN INSTRUCTIONS
Row 1 (WS): K4, p6, k2, [k1, p1] 3 times, k3, p5, k1, p1, k1, p5, k3, [p1, k1] 3 times, k2, p6, k4.
Row 2 (RS): K2, p2, k6, p2, [k1, p1] 3 times, k1, p2, k4, p1, k3, p1, k4, p2, [k1, p1] 3 times, k1, sm. p2, k6, p2, k2.
Row 3: K4, p6, k2, [k1, p1] 3 times, k3, p3, k1, p5, k1, p3, k3, [p1, k1] 3 times, k2, p6, k4.
Row 4: K2, p2, C6B, p2, [k1, p1] 3 times, k1, p2, k2, p1, k7, p1, k2, p2, [k1, p1] 3 times, k1, sm. p2, C6B, p2, k2.
Row 5: K4, p6, k2, [k1, p1] 3 times, k3, p1, k1, p9, k1, p1, k3, [p1, k1] 3 times, k2, p6, k4.
Row 6: K2, p2, k6, p2, [k1, p1] 3 times, k1, p2, k6, p1, k6, p2, [k1, p1] 3 times, k1, sm. p2, k6, p2, k2.

CHART

KEY
RS: knit
WS: purl

RS: purl
WS: knit

C6B

Next row (RS) (Place afterthought thumb): Following next row of Chart, patt 28 sts, drop yarn (do not break it), use the scrap yarn and k13 sts, break scrap yarn and without twisting slip these 13 sts back to LH ndl, pick up working yarn and patt over the 13 scrap yarn sts, patt to end.

Continue working reps of patt as set until piece measures 18cm/7" from cast-on edge, ending with row 4 of patt.

Next row (WS): K4, p2tog, p2, p2tog, k2, k1, [p1, k1] 3 times, k2, p1, k1, p9, k1, p1, k3, [p1, k1] 3 times, k2, p2tog, p2, p2tog, k4. *51 sts*

Next row: K13 then place these 13 sts on scrap yarn for button band. Leave rem 38 sts on ndl. Do not break yarn.

JOIN SIDE SEAM
With RS facing, using a 3.75mm DPN, hold work at cast-on edge and beg at first st to the left of marked st in row 1, pick up 38 sts along cast-on edge **without knitting them.**
With WS facing, hold both ndls together and using a second 3.75mm DPN, cast off all sts working a 3-needle cast off.

BUTTON BAND
Place the 13 held button band sts on a 3.75mm DPN. With WS facing, rejoin yarn – this will be next to the locking stitch marker placed in row 1.
Knit 5 rows.
Cast off and remove locking stitch marker.

AFTERTHOUGHT THUMB
Carefully remove scrap yarn and place the live sts on two DPNs, one for each side. There will be 13 sts on one side and 14 sts on the other.
With RS facing, beginning at cuff end (nearest the buttonholes), rejoin yarn, k across sts on first DPN, pick up and k1 st from gap between ndls, pm for beg of rnd, pick up and k1 st from same gap, k across sts on second DPN, pick up and k3 sts from gap (32 sts total on the ndl), then work short rows from this point as folls:

Short row 1 (RS): S1, ssk with this st and the picked up st before, turn. *31 sts*
Short row 2 (WS): Sl1, p1, p2tog, turn. *30 sts*

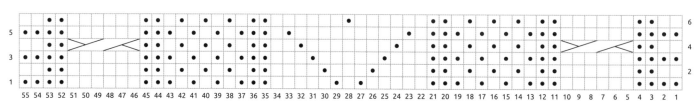

Short row 3: Sl1, k to 1 st before gap, ssk, turn. *29 sts*
Short row 4: Sl1, p to 1 st before gap, p2tog, turn. *28 sts*
Short row 5: Sl1, k to 1 st before gap, ssk, k1, turn. *1 st dec*
Short row 6: Sl1, p to 1 st before gap, p2tog, p1, turn. *1 st dec*
Rep rows 5-6 until 16 sts remain.

COMMENCE WORKING IN THE RND AGAIN:
Next rnd: K to 1 st before gap, ssk. *15 sts*
Next rnd: K2tog, k to end. *14 sts*
Knit 5 rnds.
Next rnd: *K1, p1; rep from * to end.
Next rnd: *P1, k1; rep from * to end.
Cast off in patt.

RIGHT MITT
Using 3.75mm ndls, cast on 51 sts.

Row 1 (RS): K39, place a locking stitch marker in last st worked, k to end.
Row 2 (WS) (Buttonholes): [K2, yo, k2tog] 3 times, k to end. *3 buttonholes made*

Work as for Left Mitt from ** to ***.
Next row (RS) (Place afterthought thumb): Following next row of Chart, patt 14 sts, drop yarn (do not break it), use the scrap yarn and k13 sts, break scrap yarn and without twisting slip these 13 sts back to LH ndl, pick up working yarn and patt over the 13 scrap yarn sts, patt to end.

Continue in patt as set until piece measures 18cm/7" from cast-on edge, ending with row 4 of patt.

Next row: K4, p2tog, p2, p2tog, k2, k1, [p1, k1] 3 times, k2, p1, k1, p9, k1, p1, k3, [p1, k1] 3 times, k2, p2tog, p2, p2tog, k4. *51 sts*

JOIN SIDE SEAM
With RS facing, using a 3.75mm DPN, hold work at cast-on edge and beginning at right selvedge edge, pick up 38 sts **without knitting them** along cast-on edge until you reach the marked st in row 1 but do not pick up the marked st.
With WS facing, hold both ndls together and using a second 3.75mm DPN, cast off all sts working a 3-needle cast off, then knit across rem sts – these will be the button band sts.

BUTTON BAND
Knit 5 rows.
Cast off and remove locking stitch marker.

AFTERTHOUGHT THUMB
Work thumb as for left mitt.

FINISHING
Weave in all ends. Sew top selvedge edge of button band behind the buttonhole band. Block to measurements then sew on buttons.

saltwick bay

by Graeme Knowles-Miller

Saltwick Bay is a stylish poncho combining traditional motifs from three gansey locations. At the centre of this cosy poncho, elongated moss and ladders are taken from Scarborough's simple yoke design. Further up the coast and outwards on the yoke, Robin Hood's Bay adds a simple 1x1 moss and cable column. The sides are then finished with Whitby's irrefutable signature, the Betty Martin and cables combination, so named after a well-known local with a reputation for knitting quality ganseys.

YARN USED
baa ram ewe Dovestone DK in shade: Yorkstone, 5 x 100g skeins

GAUGE
22 sts x 30 rows = 10cm/4" blocked and measured over stocking stitch on 4mm (US 6) needles

NEEDLES USED
4mm (US 6) circular needle 80cm/32"-150cm/60" lengths
3.5mm (US 4) circular needle, 60cm/24" **or** 80cm/32" **or** DPNs

OTHER SUPPLIES
Cable needle
Stitch marker

SIZING
Circumference at hem: 165cm/65"
Length: 51cm/20"

SPECIAL INSTRUCTIONS
CABLE
C4B: Slip 2 sts to cn, hold to back, k2, k2 from cn.

ABBREVIATIONS
A list of standard abbreviations appears on page 72 and also on both cover flaps.

WRITTEN INSTRUCTIONS

NECKBAND
Using 3.5mm ndls, cast on 112 sts. Join to work in the rnd, being careful not to twist and pm to indicate beg of rnd.
Rnd 1: *K2, p2; rep from * to end.
Rnd 1 sets Rib patt.
Rep rnd 1 until rib measures 5cm/2".

YOKE
Change to shorter 4mm ndl, swapping to longer ndl as the stitch count increases, and work as foll:

Rnd 1: [P1, k4, p1, k22, pm] 4 times.
Rnd 2: [P1, k4, p1, m1p, p to m, m1p, sm] 4 times. *120 sts*
Rnd 3: [P1, k4, p1, k to m, sm] 4 times.
Rnd 4: [P1, k4, p1, m1p, p to m, m1p, sm] 4 times. *128 sts*
Rnd 5: [P1, k4, p1, k to m, sm] 4 times.
Rnd 6: [P1, k4, p1, m1r, k to m, m1l, sm] 4 times. *136 sts*
Rnd 7: [P1, k4, p1, k to m, sm] 4 times.
Rnd 8: [P1, C4B, p1, m1r, k to m, m1l, sm] 4 times. *144 sts*
Rnd 9: [P1, k4, p1, k to m, sm] 4 times.
Rnd 10: [P1, k4, p1, m1r, k to m, m1l, sm] 4 times. *152 sts*
Rnd 11: [P1, k4, p1, k to m, sm] 4 times.
Rnd 12: [P1, k4, p1, m1r, k to m, m1l, sm] 4 times. *160 sts*
Rnd 13: [P1, C4B, p1, k to m, sm] 4 times.
Rnd 14: [P1, k4, p1, m1r, k to m, m1l, sm] 4 times. *168 sts*
Rnd 15: [P1, k4, p1, k to m, sm] 4 times.
Rnd 16: [P1, k4, p1, m1r, k to m, m1l, sm] 4 times. *176 sts*
Rnd 17: [P1, k4, p1, k to m, sm] 4 times.
Rnd 18: [P1, C4B, p1, m1r, k to m, m1l, sm] 4 times. *184 sts*

Rnds 19-38: Rep rnds 9-18 twice more. *264 sts*

Rnd 39: [P1, k4, p1, k to m, sm] 4 times.
Rnd 40: [P1, k4, p1, m1p, p to m, m1p, sm] 4 times. *272 sts*
Rnd 41: [P1, k4, p1, k to m, sm] 4 times.
Rnd 42: [P1, k4, p1, m1p, p to m, m1p, sm] 4 times. *280 sts*
Rnd 43: [P1, C4B, p1, k to m, sm] 4 times.

BODY

Reading from the Chart or Written Instructions below, work rnds 1-50 working the rep 4 times across the rnd.

CHART - WRITTEN INSTRUCTIONS

Rnd 1: *P1, k4, p1, m1p, [k1, p1] 5 times, k4, p1, k12, [p2, k2] 3 times, k10, p1, k4, [p1, k1] 5 times, m1p, sm; rep from * a further 3 times. *288 sts*
Rnd 2: *P1, k4, p3, [k1, p1] 4 times, p1, k4, p1, k10, [p2, k2] 3 times, p2, k10, p1, k4, p2, [k1, p1] 3 times, k1, p2; rep from * a further 3 times.
Rnd 3: *P1, k4, p1, m1r, [p1, k1] 5 times, p1, k4, p11, [k2, p2] 3 times, k2, p11, k4, p1, [k1, p1] 5 times, m1l; rep from * a further 3 times. *296 sts*
Rnd 4: *P1, k4, p1, k1, p2, [k1, p1] 3 times, k1, p2, p4, k4, p13, [k2, p2] 2 times, k2, p13, k4, p2, [k1, p1] 4 times, p1, k1; rep from * a further 3 times.
Rnd 5: *P1, C4B, p1, m1r, [k1, p1] 6 times, C4B, p1, k12, [p2, k2] twice, p2, k12, p1, C4B, [p1, k1] 6 times, m1l; rep from * a further 3 times. *304 sts*
Rnd 6: *P1, k4, p1, k2, p2, [k1, p1] 3 times, k1, p2, k4, p1, k10, [p2, k2] 3 times, p2, k10, p1, k4, p2, [k1, p1] 3 times, k1, p2, k2; rep from * a further 3 times.
Rnd 7: *P1, k4, p1, m1r, k2, [p1, k1] 5 times, p1, k4, p11, [k2, p2] 3 times, k2, p11, k4, [p1, k1] 5 times, p1, k2, m1l; rep from * a further 3 times. *312 sts*
Rnd 8: *P1, k4, p1, k3, p2, [k1, p1] 3 times, k1, p2, k4, p13, [k2, p2] twice, k2, p13, k4, p2, [k1, p1] 3 times, k1, p2, k3; rep from * a further 3 times.
Rnd 9: *P1, k4, p1, m1r, k3, [p1, k1] 5 times, p1, k4, p1, k12, [p2, k2] twice, p2, k12, p1, k4, [p1, k1] 5 times, p1, k3, m1l; rep from * a further 3 times. *320 sts*
Rnd 10: *P1, C4B, p1, k4, p2, [k1, p1] 3 times, k1, p2, C4B, p1, k10, [p2, k2] 3 times, p2, k10, p1, C4B, p2, [k1, p1] 3 times, k1, p2, k4; rep from * a further 3 times.
Rnd 11: *P1, k4, p1, m1p, k4, [p1, k1] 5 times, p1, k4, p11, [k2, p2] 3 times, k2, p11, k4, [p1, k1] 5 times, p1, k4, m1p; rep from * a further 3 times. *328 sts*
Rnd 12: *P1, k4, p2, k4, p2, [k1, p1] 3 times, k1, p2, k4, p13, [k2, p2] twice, k2, p13, k4, p2, [k1, p1] 3 times, k1, p2, k4, p1; rep from * a further 3 times.
Rnd 13: *P1, k4, p1, m1r, p1, k4, [p1, k1] 5 times, p1, k4, p1, k12, [p2, k2] twice, p2, k12, p1, k4, [p1, k1] 5 times, p1, k4, p1, m1l; rep from * a further 3 times. *336 sts*

Rnd 14: *P1, k4, p1, k1, p1, k4, p2, [k1, p1] 3 times, k1, p2, k4, p1, k10, [p2, k2] 3 times, p2, k10, p1, k4, p2, [k1, p1] 3 times, k1, p2, k4, p1, k1; rep from * a further 3 times.
Rnd 15: *P1, C4B, p1, m1r, k1, p1, C4B, [p1, k1] 5 times, p1, C4B, p11, [k2, p2] 3 times, k2, p11, C4B, [p1, k1] 5 times, p1, C4B, p1, k1, m1l; rep from * a further 3 times. *344 sts*
Rnd 16: *P1, k4, p1, k2, p1, k4, p2, [k1, p1] 3 times, k1, p2, k4, p13, [k2, p2] twice, k2, p13, k4, p2, [k1, p1] 3 times, k1, p2, k4, p1, k2; rep from * a further 3 times.
Rnd 17: *P1, k4, p1, m1r, k2, p1, k4, [p1, k1] 5 times, p1, k4, p1, k12, [p2, k2] twice, p2, k12, p1, k4, [p1, k1] 5 times, p1, k4, p1, k2, m1l; rep from * a further 3 times. *352 sts*
Rnd 18: *P1, k4, p1, k3, p1, k4, p2, [k1, p1] 3 times, k1, p2, k4, p1, k10, [p2, k2] 3 times, p2, k10, p1, k4, p2, [k1, p1] 3 times, k1, p2, k4, p1, k3; rep from * a further 3 times.
Rnd 19: *P1, k4, p1, m1p, p1, k2, p1, k4, [p1, k1] 5 times, p1, k4, p11, [k2, p2] 3 times, k2, p11, k4, [p1, k1] 5 times, p1, k4, p1, k2, p1, m1p; rep from * a further 3 times. *360 sts*
Rnd 20: *P1, C4B, p3, k2, p1, C4B, p2, [k1, p1] 3 times, k1, p2, C4B, p13, [k2, p2] twice, k2, p13, C4B, p2, [k1, p1] 3 times, k1, p2, C4B, p1, k2, p2; rep from * a further 3 times.
Rnd 21: *P1, k4, p1, m1r, k4, p1, k4, [p1, k1] 5 times, p1, k4, p1, k12, [p2, k2] twice, p2, k12, p1, k4, [p1, k1] 5 times, p1, k4, p1, k4, m1l; rep from * a further 3 times. *368 sts*
Rnd 22: *P1, k4, p1, k5, p1, k4, p2, [k1, p1] 3 times, k1, p2, k4, p1, k10, [p2, k2] 3 times, p2, k10, p1, k4, p2, [k1, p1] 3 times, k1, p2, k4, p1, k5; rep from * a further 3 times.
Rnd 23: *P1, k4, p1, m1r, k1, p2, k2, p1, k4, [p1, k1] 5 times, p1, k4, p11, [k2, p2] 3 times, k2, p11, k4, [p1, k1] 5 times, p1, k4, p1, k2, p2, k1, m1l; rep from * a further 3 times. *376 sts*
Rnd 24: *P1, k4, p1, k2, p2, k2, p1, k4, p2, [k1, p1] 3 times, k1, p2, k4, p13, [k2, p2] twice, k2, p13, k4, p2, [k1, p1] 3 times, k1, p2, k4, p1, k2, p2, k2; rep from * a further 3 times.
Rnd 25: *P1, C4B, p1, m1r, k6, p1, C4B, [p1, k1] 5 times, p1, C4B, p1, k12, [p2, k2] twice, p2, k12, p1, C4B, [p1, k1] 5 times, p1, C4B, p1, k6, m1l; rep from * a further 3 times. *384 sts*
Rnd 26: *P1, k4, p1, k7, p1, k4, p2, [k1, p1] 3 times, k1, p2, k4, p1, k10, [p2, k2] 3 times, p2, k10, p1, k4, p2, [k1, p1] 3 times, k1, p2, k4, p1, k7; rep from * a further 3 times.
Rnd 27: *P1, k1, p1, m1p, p1, k2, p2, k2, p1, k4, [p1, k1] 5 times, p1, k4, p11, [k2, p2] 3 times, k2, p11, k4, [p1, k1] 5 times, p1, k4, p1, k2, p2, k2, p1, m1p; rep from * a further 3 times. *392 sts*
Rnd 28: *P1, k4, p3, k2, p2, k2, p1, k4, p2, [k1, p1] 3 times, k1, p2, k4, p13, [k2, p2] twice, k2, p13, k4, p2, [k1, p1] 3 times, k1, p2, k4, p1, [k2, p2] twice; rep from * a further 3 times.
Rnd 29: *P1, k4, p1, m1r, k8, p1, k4, [p1, k1] 5 times, p1, k4, p1, k12, [p2, k2] twice, p2, k12, p1, k4, [p1, k1] 5 times, p1, k4, p1, k8, m1l; rep from * a further 3 times. *400 sts*
Rnd 30: *P1, C4B, p1, k9, p1, C4B, p2, [k1, p1] 3 times, k1, p2, C4B, p1, k10, [p2, k2] 3 times, p2, k10, p1, C4B, p2, [k1, p1] 3 times, k1, p2, C4B, p1, k9; rep from * a further 3 times.
Rnd 31: *P1, k4, p1, m1r, k1, [p2, k2] twice, p1, k4, [p1, k1] 5 times, p1, k4, p11, [k2, p2] 3 times, k2, p11, k4, [p1, k1] 5

times, p1, k4, p1, [k2, p2] twice k1, m1l; rep from * a further 3 times. *408 sts*

Rnd 32: *P1, k4, p1, [k2, p2] twice, k2, p1, k4, p2, [k1, p1] 3 times, k1, p2, k4, p13, [k2, p2] twice, k2, p13, k4, p2, [k1, p1] 3 times, k1, p2, k4, p1, [k2, p2] twice, k2; rep from * a further 3 times.

Rnd 33: *P1, k4, p1, m1r, k10, p1, k4, [p1, k1] 5 times, p1, k4, p1, k12, [p2, k2] twice, p2, k12, p1, k4, [p1, k1] 5 times, p1, k4, p1, k10, m1l; rep from * a further 3 times. *416 sts*

Rnd 34: *P1, k4, p1, k11, p1, k4, p2, [k1, p1] 3 times, k1, p2, k4, p1, k10, [p2, k2] 3 times, p2, k10, p1, k4, p2, [k1, p1] 3 times, k1, p2, k4, p1, k11; rep from * a further 3 times.

Rnd 35: *P1, C4B, p1, m1r, p1, [k2, p2] twice, k2, p1, C4B, [p1, k1] 5 times, p1, C4B, p11, [k2, p2] 3 times, k2, p11, C4B, [p1, k1] 5 times, p1, C4B, p1, [k2, p2] twice, k2, p1, m1l; rep from * a further 3 times. *424 sts*

Rnd 36: *P1, k4, p3, [k2, p2] twice, k2, p1, k4, p2, [k1, p1] 3 times, k1, p2, k4, p13, [k2, p2] twice, k2, p13, k4, p2, [k1, p1] 3 times, k1, p2, k4, p1, [k2, p2] 3 times; rep from * a further 3 times.

Rnd 37: *P1, k4, p1, m1r, k12, p1, k4, [p1, k1] 5 times, p1, k4, p1, k12, [p2, k2] twice, p2, k12, p1, k4, [p1, k1] 5 times, p1, k4, p1, k12, m1l; rep from * a further 3 times. *432 sts*

Rnd 38: *P1, k4, p1, k13, p1, k4, p2, [k1, p1] 3 times, k1, p2, k4, p1, k10, [p2, k2] 3 times, p2, k10, p1, k4, p2, [k1, p1] 3 times, k1, p2, k4, p1, k13; rep from * a further 3 times.

Rnd 39: *P1, k4, p1, m1r, k1, [p2, k2] 3 times, p1, k4, [p1, k1] 5 times, p1, k4, p11, [k2, p2] 3 times, k2, p11, k4, [p1, k1] 5 times, p1, k4, p1, [k2, p2] 3 times, k1, m1l; rep from * a further 3 times. *440 sts*

Rnd 40: *P1, C4B, p1, [k2, p2] 3 times, k2, p1, C4B, p2, [k1, p1] 3 times, k1, p2, C4B, p13, [k2, p2] twice, k2, p13, C4B, p2, [k1, p1] 3 times, k1, p2, C4B, p1, [k2, p2] 3 times, k2; rep from * a further 3 times.

Rnd 41: *P1, k4, p1, m1r, k14, p1, k4, [p1, k1] 5 times, p1, k4, p1, k12, [p2, k2] twice, p2, k12, p1, k4, [p1, k1] 5 times, p1, k4, p1, k14, m1l; rep from * a further 3 times. *448 sts*

Rnd 42: *P1, k4, p1, k15, p1, k4, p2, [k1, p1] 3 times, k1, p2, k4, p1, k10, [p2, k2] 3 times, p2, k10, p1, k4, p2, [k1, p1] 3 times, k1, p2, k4, p1, k15; rep from * a further 3 times.

Rnd 43: *P1, k4, p1, m1p, p1, [k2, p2] 3 times, k2, p1, k4, [p1, k1] 5 times, p1, k4, p11, [k2, p2] 3 times, k2, p11, k4, [p1, k1] 5 times, p1, k4, p1, [k2, p2] 3 times, k2, p1, m1p; rep from * a further 3 times. *456 sts*

Rnd 44: *P1, k4, p3, [k2, p2] 3 times, k2, p1, k4, p2, [k1, p1] 3 times, k1, p2, k4, p13, [k2, p2] twice, k2, p13, k4, p2, [k1, p1] 3 times, k1, p2, k4, p1, [k2, p2] 4 times; rep from * a further 3 times.

Rnd 45: *P1, C4B, p1, m1r, k16, p1, C4B, [p1, k1] 5 times, p1, C4B, p1, k12, [p2, k2] twice, p2, k12, p1, C4B, [p1, k1] 5 times, p1, C4B, p1, k16, m1l; rep from * a further 3 times. *464 sts*

Rnd 46: *P1, k4, p1, k17, p1, k4, p2, [k1, p1] 3 times, k1, p2, k4, p1, k10, [p2, k2] 3 times, p2, k10, p1, k4, p2, [k1, p1] 3 times, k1, p2, k4, p1, k17; rep from * a further 3 times.

Rnd 47: *P1, k4, p1 m1r, k1, [p2, k2] 4 times, p1, k4, [p1, k1] 5 times, p1, k4, p11, [k2, p2] 3 times, k2, p11, k4, [p1, k1] 5 times, p1, k4, p1, [k2, p2] 4 times, k1, m1l; rep from * a further 3 times. *472 sts*

Rnd 48: *P1, k4, p1, [k2, p2] 4 times, k2, p1, k4, p2, [k1, p1] 3 times, k1, p2, k4, p13, [k2, p2] twice, k2, p13, k4, p2, [k1, p1] 3 times, k1, p2, k4, p1, [k2, p2] 4 times, k2; rep from * a further 3 times.

Rnd 49: *P1, k4, p1, m1r, k18, p1, k4, [p1, k1] 5 times, p1, k4, p1, k12, [p2, k2] twice, p2, k12, p1, k4, [p1, k1] 5 times, p1, k4, p1, k18, m1l; rep from * a further 3 times. *480 sts*

Rnd 50: *P1, C4B, k19, p1, k2tog, k2, p2, [k1, p1] 3 times, k1, p2, k2tog, k2, p1, k10, [p2, k2] 3 times, p2, k10, p1, k2tog, k2, p2, [k1, p1] 3 times, k1, p2, k2tog, k2, p1, k19; rep from * a further 3 times. *464 sts*

Rnd 51: [P1, k4, p to m] 4 times.
Rnd 52: [P1, k4, p1, m1r, k to m, m1l] 4 times. *472 sts*
Rnds 53-54: Rep rnds 51-52 once more. *480 sts*
Rnd 55: [P1, C4B, p1, k to m] 4 times.
Rnd 56: [P1, k4, p1, m1r, k to m, m1l] 4 times. *488 sts*
Rnd 57: [P1, k4, p1, k to m] 4 times.
Rnds 58-59: Rep rnds 56-57. *496 sts*
Rnd 60: [P1, C4B, p1, m1r, k to m, m1l] 4 times. *504 sts*
Rnd 61: [P1, k4, p1, k to m] 4 times.
Rnd 62: [P1, k4, p1, m1r, k to m, m1l] 4 times. *512 sts*
Rnd 63-64: Rep rnds 61-62. *520 sts*
Work reps of rnds 55-64, continuing to inc as set until piece measures 56cm/22" from cast-on edge.
Cast off loosely.

FINISHING
Weave in ends and block flat in a square shape, pulling the corners into sharp points. The cast-off edge will curl lightly when dry.

SALTWICK BAY

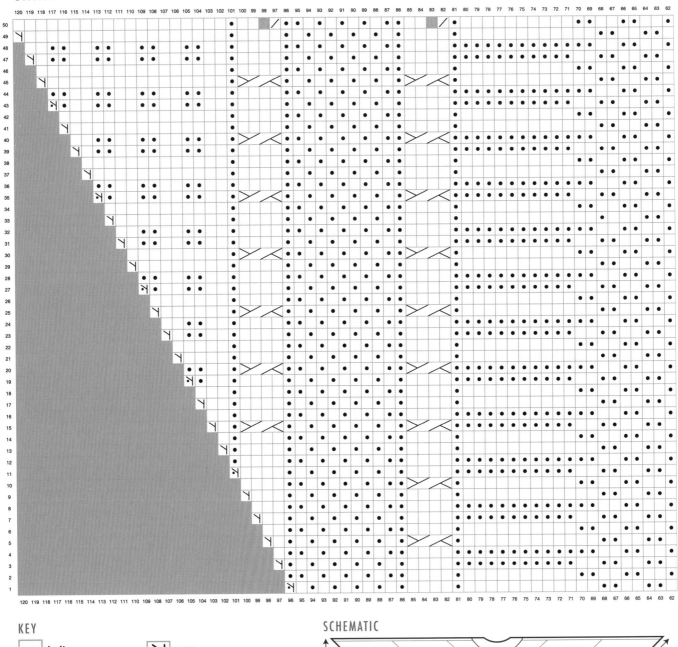

KEY

☐	knit
•	purl
▨	no stitch
↗	m1r
↗•	m1p

↖	m1l
↖•	m1p
⤬	C4B
╱	k2tog

SCHEMATIC

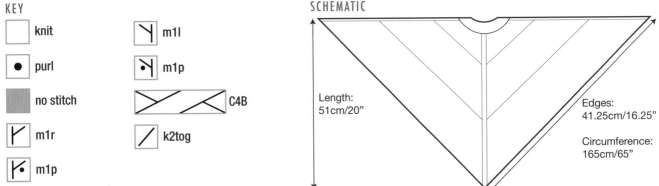

Length:
51cm/20"

Edges:
41.25cm/16.25"

Circumference:
165cm/65"

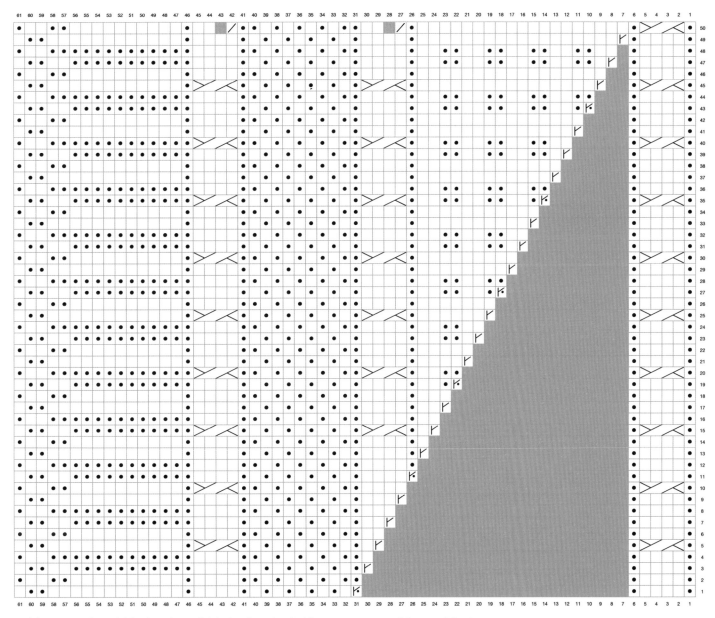

A larger version of this chart is available for download at **baaramewe.co.uk/pages/charts**

flamborough

by Alison Moreton

An A-line open-fronted cardigan with moss stitch edges and a collar in cable, moss and net mask patterns inspired by 'Flamborough Pattern I' in *Patterns for Guernseys, Jerseys and Arans*. Flamborough is where most of my childhood seaside trips were taken: my grandfather spent his early childhood there when his father (my great-grandfather) was vicar of St Oswald's Flamborough in the 1920s and early 1930s.

PATTERN NOTES

In the original Flamborough Pattern I, the cable was crossed every 7th row. I have specified crossing every 6th row (sizes XS-M) or 8th row (sizes L-3XL) to fit with the repeat of the net mask chart, but you can choose to cross the cable every 7th row if preferred.

SIZING

XS (S, M, L, XL, 2XL, 3XL) (see sizing table for more info)

YARN USED

baa ram ewe Dovestone DK in shade:
Aire, 4 (5, 5, 5, 6, 6, 7) x 100g skeins

GAUGE

22 sts x 30 rows = 10cm/4" blocked and measured over stocking stitch on 4mm (US 6) needles

NEEDLES USED

3.75mm (US 5) circular needle 80cm/32" or longer
3.75mm (US 5) DPNs
4mm (US 6) circular needle 40cm/16" length
4mm (US 6) circular needle 80cm/32" or longer
4mm (US 6) DPNs

OTHER SUPPLIES

Cable needle
Stitch markers
4 locking stitch markers (1 in a different colour)
Stitch holders or scrap yarn

SIZING TABLE

	xs	s	m	l	xl	2xl	3xl	
TO FIT BUST								
	71-76	81-86	91.5-96.5	101.5-106.5	111.5-117	122-127	132-137	cm
	28-30	32-34	36-38	40-42	44-46	48-50	52-54	in
FINISHED BUST – A ON SCHEMATIC								
	81.5	91.5	101.5	112	122	132	142	cm
	32	36	40	44	48	52	56	in
CROSS BACK – B ON SCHEMATIC								
	33	34.5	37	38	40.5	43	45.4	cm
	13	13½	14½	15	16	17	18	in
HIP – C ON SCHEMATIC								
	91.5	101.5	112	122	132	145	155	cm
	36	40	44	48	52	57	61	in
ARMHOLE DEPTH – D ON SCHEMATIC								
	19	20.5	21.5	23	24	25.5	26.5	cm
	7½	8	8½	9	9½	10	10½	in
UNDERARM TO BOTTOM EDGE – E ON SCHEMATIC								
	41.5	41.5	41.5	41.5	41.5	41.5	41.5	cm
	16¼	16¼	16¼	16¼	16¼	16¼	16¼	in
FULL LENGTH – F ON SCHEMATIC								
	61.5	63	64	65.5	66.5	68	69	cm
	24¼	24¾	25¼	25¾	26¼	26.75	27¼	in
NECK WIDTH – G ON SCHEMATIC								
	12.5	14	15	16.5	16.5	18	18	cm
	5	5½	6	6½	6½	7	7	in
SHOULDER WIDTH – H ON SCHEMATIC								
	10	10	11	11	12	12.5	14	cm
	4	4	4¼	4¼	4¾	5	5½	in
UPPER ARM – I ON SCHEMATIC								
	27.5	28.5	30.5	33	36.5	42	45.5	cm
	10¾	11¼	12	13	14½	16½	18	in
CUFF – J ON SCHEMATIC								
	21.5	21.5	23	23	24	24	25.5	cm
	8½	8½	9	9	9½	9½	10	in
SLEEVE LENGTH UNDERARM TO CUFF – K ON SCHEMATIC								
	42	43	43	44.5	44.5	46	46	cm
	16½	17	17	17½	17½	18	18	in

SPECIAL INSTRUCTIONS
CABLE
C6B: Slip 3 sts to cn and hold in back, k3, k3 from cn

ABBREVIATIONS
A list of standard abbreviations appears on page 72 and also on both cover flaps.

HINTS AND TIPS
It is really important to cast off for the back neck, rather than using the live sts to work the collar. The cast-off edge will stabilise the neck and stop it stretching out of shape. Likewise, don't be tempted to graft the shoulders for the same reason.

I suggest joining new yarn in the stocking stitch body of the cardigan rather than at the ends of rows, to make it easier to maintain neat edges. Dovestone DK is very easy to splice together with a felted join.

CHARTS: WRITTEN INSTRUCTIONS

FLAMBOROUGH CABLE: RIGHT SET-UP
Row 1 (RS): P1, k1, [p1, k3] twice, p1, k1.
Row 2 (WS): K1, p1, [k1, p3] twice, k1, p1.
Rows 3-4: Rep rows 1-2.
Row 5: P1, k1, p1, k7, p1, k1.
Row 6: K1, p1, k1, p7, k1, p1.
Row 7: P1, k1, m1, p1, C6B, p1, m1, p1, k1. *14 sts*
Row 8: P2, k2, p6, k2, p2.

FLAMBOROUGH CABLE: LEFT SET-UP
Row 1 (RS): K1, [p1, k3] twice, p1, k1, p1.
Row 2 (WS): P1, [k1, p3] twice, k1, p1, k1.
Rows 3-4: Rep rows 1-2.
Row 5: K1, p1, k7, p1, k1, p1.
Row 6: P1, k1, p7, k1, p1, k1.
Row 7: K1, p1, m1, p1, C6B, p1, m1, k1, p1. *14 sts*
Row 8: P2, k2, p6, k2, p2.

FLAMBOROUGH CABLE: FOR SIZES XS TO M
Row 1 (RS): K2, p2, k6, p2, k2.
Row 2 (WS and all following WS rows): P2, k2, p6, k2, p2.
Row 3: Rep row 1.
Row 5: K2, p2, C6B, p2, k2.
Rep rows 1-6 for pattern.

FLAMBOROUGH CABLE: FOR SIZES L-3XL
Row 1 (RS): K2, p2, k6, p2, k2.
Row 2 (WS and all following WS rows): P2, k2, p6, k2, p2.
Row 3: Rep row 1.
Row 5: Rep row 1.
Row 7: K2, p2, C6B, p2, k2.
Rep rows 1-8 for pattern.

13 STITCH NET MASK CHART: FOR SIZES XS-M
Row 1 (RS): Knit.
Row 2 (WS): Purl.
Row 3: Knit.
Row 4: P6, k1, p6.
Row 5: K5, p1, k1, p1, k5.
Row 6: P4, [k1, p1] twice, k1, p4.
Row 7: K3, [p1, k1] 3 times, p1, k3.
Row 8: P2, [k1, p1] 4 times, k1, p2.
Row 9: [K1, p1] 6 times, k1.
Row 10: Rep row 8.
Row 11: Rep row 7.
Row 12: Rep row 6.
Row 13: Rep row 5.
Row 14: Rep row 4.
Rep rows 3-14 for pattern.

15 STITCH NET MASK CHART FOR SIZES: L-3XL
Row 1 (RS): Knit.
Row 2 (WS): Purl.
Row 3: Knit.
Row 4: P7, k1, p7.
Row 5: K6, p1, k1, p1, k6.
Row 6: P5, [k1, p1] twice, k1, p5.
Row 7: K4, [p1, k1] 3 times, p1, k4.
Row 8: P3, [k1, p1] 4 times, k1, p3.
Row 9: K2, [p1, k1] 5 times, p1, k2.
Row 10: [P1, k1] 7 times, p1.
Row 11: Rep row 9.
Row 12: Rep row 8.
Row 13: Rep row 7.
Row 14: Rep row 6.
Row 15: Rep row 5.
Row 16: Rep row 4.
Rep rows 1-16 for pattern.

CHARTS

KEY

- ☐ RS: knit / WS: purl
- ● RS: purl / WS: knit
- ♉ RS: m1
- ✕ C6B
- ☐ repeat

FLAMBOROUGH CABLE: LEFT SET UP

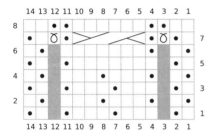

FLAMBOROUGH CABLE: RIGHT SET UP

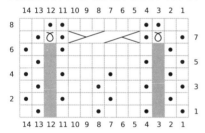

FLAMBOROUGH CABLE: XS-M

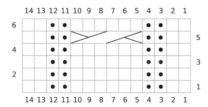

FLAMBOROUGH CABLE: L-3XL

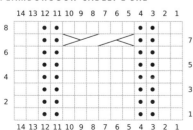

BODY

Using 3.75mm ndl, cast on 197 (221, 241, 265, 289, 317, 337) sts. Do not join.

Work flat in rows as foll:

Moss row 1 (RS): Sl1 wyif, *k1, p1; rep from * to last 2 sts, k1, k1tbl.

Moss row 2 (WS): Sl1 wyif, *k1, p1; rep from * to last 2 sts, k1, k1tbl.

Rep rows 1-2 a further 5 times.

Change to 4mm ndl.

Row 1 (RS): Sl1 wyif, moss 20 sts as set, pm, k28 (34, 39, 45, 51, 58, 63), pm, k99 (111, 121, 133, 145, 159, 169), pm, k28 (34, 39, 45, 51, 58, 63), pm, moss 20 sts as set, k1tbl.

Row 2 (WS): Patt to m, sm, p to last m, sm, patt to end.

Rep rows 1-2, slipping the markers as you pass them, until piece measures 13cm/5" from cast-on edge ending with a WS row.

Dec row (RS): Patt to m, sm, [k to 5 sts before m, ssk, k to m, sm, k3, k2tog] twice, k to m, sm, patt to end. *4 sts dec*

Work 13 (13, 13, 13, 11, 9, 9) rows straight.

Rep last 14 (14, 14, 14, 12, 10, 10) rows a further 4 (4, 4, 4, 5, 6, 6) times. *177 (201, 221, 245, 265, 289, 309) sts*

Work straight until piece measures 41cm/16¼" from cast-on edge, ending with a WS row.

13 STITCH NET MASK CHART: XS-M

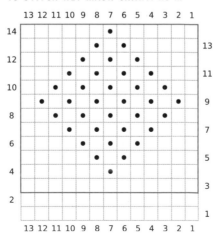

15 STITCH NET MASK CHART: L-3XL

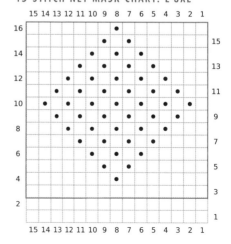

SEPARATE FRONTS AND BACK

Patt to m, sm, k to 3 (4, 4, 5, 6, 7, 7) sts before m, slip next 6 (8, 8, 10, 12, 14, 14) sts to stitch holder for underarm. Leaving working yarn attached, join a new ball of yarn to work the back.

BACK

K to 3 (4, 4, 5, 6, 7, 7) sts before m, slip next 6 (8, 8, 10, 12, 14, 14) sts to stitch holder for underarm, turn.
Back is worked over these 83 (93, 103, 113, 121, 131, 141) sts.

Next row (WS): Purl.

Continue to work in St st throughout the back and shape as foll:

SIZES S-3XL ONLY
Cast off – (2, 2, 3, 3, 3, 4) sts at beg of next 2 rows. – *(89, 99, 107, 115, 125, 133) sts*

SIZES L-3XL ONLY
Cast off – (–, –, 2, 2, 3, 3) sts at beg of next 2 rows. – *(–, –, 103, 111, 119, 127) sts*

ALL SIZES AGAIN
Row 1 (RS): K2, ssk, work to 4 sts before end, k2tog, k2. *2 sts dec*
Row 2 (WS): Purl.
Rep these 2 rows a further 4 (5, 8, 8, 10, 11, 13) times. *73 (77, 81, 85, 89, 95, 99) sts*

Work straight until back measures 19 (20.5, 21.5, 23, 24, 25.5, 26.5)cm/7½ (8, 8½, 9, 9½, 10, 10½)" from underarm.

SHAPE SHOULDERS WITH SHORT ROWS AS FOLL:
Short row 1 (RS): K to 4 (4, 4, 4, 5, 5, 5) sts from end, w&t.
Short row 2 (WS): P24 (25, 27, 29, 30, 33, 35), w&t.
Short row 3: K to 11 (11, 11, 12, 13, 14, 15) sts from end, w&t.
Short row 4: P14 (15, 16, 17, 18, 19, 20), w&t.
Short row 5: K to 18 (18, 18, 20, 21, 23, 25) sts from end, w&t.

Short row 6: P51 (55, 59, 61, 63, 67, 69), w&t.
Short row 7: K24 (25, 27, 29, 30, 33, 35) w&t.
Short row 8: P to 11 (11, 11, 12, 13, 14, 15) sts from end.
Short row 9: K14 (15, 16, 17, 18, 19, 20), w&t.
Short row 10: P to 18 (18, 18, 20, 21, 23, 25) sts from end, w&t.
Short row 11: K to end, picking up wraps and working together with the sts they wrap.
Next row (WS): P23 (25, 24, 25, 27, 29, 31), using the last st worked as the first st to cast off, cast off 29 (33, 35, 37, 37, 39, 39) sts for neck, p to end.

Slip rem 22 (22, 23, 24, 26, 28, 30) sts each side of neck to stitch holders for shoulders.

RIGHT FRONT
Front is worked over 41 (46, 51, 56, 60, 65, 70) sts. Working yarn will still be attached at armhole edge.

Beg with a WS row, work 2 rows straight, maintaining moss st as set at neck edge.

Continue to work neck edge in moss st throughout and work shaping as foll:
Note: Where 'patt' is referred to this includes the moss st band with St st across the remaining sts of the row.

SIZES S–3XL ONLY
Next row (WS): Cast off – (2, 2, 3, 3, 3, 4) sts, p to m, sm, patt to end. – *(44, 49, 53, 57, 62, 66) sts*
Next row (RS): Patt to m, k to end.

SIZES L–3XL ONLY
Next row (WS): Cast off – (– , –, 2, 2, 3, 3) sts, p to m, sm, patt to end. – *(–, –, 51, 55, 59, 63) sts*
Next row (RS): Patt to m, k to end.

ALL SIZES AGAIN
Dec row (RS): Patt to 3 sts from end, k2tog, k1. *1 st dec*
Work 1 row straight.
Rep last 2 rows a further 6 (7, 10, 10, 12, 13, 15) times. *34 (36, 38, 40, 42, 45, 47) sts*

Work straight until front is 4 rows shorter than back from underarm at this point, measuring at armhole edge and ending with a WS row.

Next row (RS): Patt to m, sm, k to last 2 sts, m1l, k2. *1 st inc*
Work 1 row straight.
Rep last 2 rows once more. *36 (38, 40, 42, 44, 47, 49) sts*

SHAPE SHOULDERS WITH SHORT ROWS AS FOLL:
Short row 1 (RS): Patt to m, sm, k to last 4 (4, 4, 4, 5, 5, 5) sts, w&t.
Short row 2 (WS): Patt to end.
Short row 3: Patt to m, sm, k to last 11 (11, 11, 12, 13, 14, 15) sts, w&t.
Short row 4: Patt to end.
Short row 5: Patt to m, sm, k to last 18 (18, 18, 20, 21, 23, 25) sts, w&t.
Short row 6: Patt to end.
Next row (RS): Patt to m, sm, k to end, picking up wraps and working together with the sts they wrap.

Slip 22 (22, 23, 24, 26, 28, 30) sts right back shoulder sts onto a spare ndl, hold with RS sides together and work 3-needle cast off, working rem 14 (16, 17, 18, 18, 19, 19) sts for right front in patt to end. Leave yarn attached, or if you wish to break yarn, leave a long tail (this will allow you to join new yarn at the middle of the collar rather than at the edge) and place sts on a stitch holder.

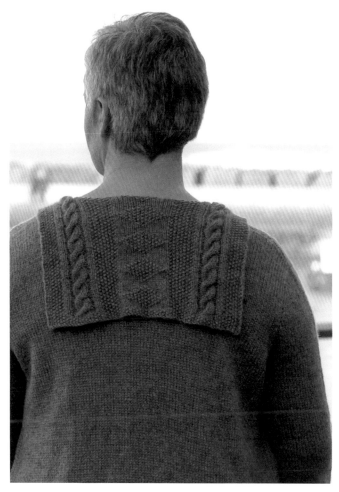

LEFT FRONT

With RS facing, rejoin yarn at armhole edge. Front is worked over 41 (46, 51, 56, 60, 65, 70) sts.

Beg with a RS row, work 2 rows straight, maintaining moss st as set at neck edge.

Continue to work neck edge in moss st throughout and work shaping as foll:
Note: Where 'patt' is referred to this includes the moss st band with St st across the rem sts.

SIZES S-3XL ONLY
Next row (RS): Cast off – (2, 2, 3, 3, 3, 4) sts, k to m, sm, patt to end. – (44, 49, 53, 57, 62, 66) sts
Next row (WS): Patt to m, sm, p to end.

SIZES L-3XL ONLY
Next row (RS): Cast off – (–, –, 2, 2, 3, 3) sts, k to m, sm, patt to end. – (–, –, 51, 55, 59, 63) sts
Next row (WS): Patt to m, sm, p to end.

ALL SIZES AGAIN
Dec row (RS): K2, ssk, k to m, sm, patt to end.
Work 1 row straight.
Rep last 2 rows a further 6 (7, 10, 10, 12, 13, 15) times. 34 (36, 38, 40, 42) sts

Work straight until front is 4 rows shorter than back from underarm at this point, measuring at armhole edge and ending with a WS row.

Next row (RS): K2, m1l, k to m, sm, patt to end, k2. *1 st inc*
Work 1 row straight.
Rep last 2 rows once more. 36 (38, 40, 42, 44, 47, 49) sts

SHAPE SHOULDERS WITH SHORT ROWS AS FOLL:
Short row 1 (RS): Patt to m, sm, p to last 4 (4, 4, 4, 5, 5, 5) sts, w&t.
Short row 2 (WS): Patt to end.
Short row 3: Patt to m, sm, p to last 11 (11, 11, 12, 13, 14, 15) sts, w&t.
Short row 4: Patt to end.
Short row 5: Patt to m, sm, p to last 18 (18, 18, 20, 21, 23, 25) sts, w&t
Short row 6: Patt to end.
Next row (RS): Patt to m, sm, p to end, picking up wraps and working together with the sts they wrap.
Next row (WS): Patt to end.
Next row: Patt 14 (16, 17, 18, 18, 19, 19) sts, then join left shoulder as foll: Place rem 22 (22, 23, 24, 26, 28, 30) left back sts on a spare ndl and holding RS sides together, work a 3-needle cast off to join the shoulder.

COLLAR

With RS facing, slip 14 (16, 17, 18, 18, 19, 19) held right neck edge sts onto a spare ndl. Using 3.75mm ndl, patt across these sts, pick up and k29 (33, 31, 31, 39, 37, 37) sts across neck, then patt across sts left neck edge sts remaining on ndl from body. 57 (65, 65, 67, 75, 75, 75) sts

Note: Foll row becomes first RS row of collar – WS of neck edges fold back and become RS of collar.

Next row: Patt 5 (7, 7, 7, 9, 9, 9) sts, pm, work Flamborough Cable Left Set-up over next 12 sts, pm, moss 5 (7, 7, 7, 9, 9, 9) sts, continuing in patt from last 2 sts of cable set-up chart, pm, working the correct Net Mask Chart for your size work across next 13 (13, 13, 15, 15, 15, 15) sts, pm, starting with a knit st work moss across 5 (7, 7, 7, 9, 9, 9) sts, pm, work Flamborough Cable Right Set-up over next 12 sts, pm, patt to end.

Continue to work collar in patt as set. Once cable set-up chart rows have been completed, switch to cable chart for XS-M or L-3XL as appropriate.

Work collar until it measures 19.5cm/7½" from neck edge, ending with last row of Net Mask Chart.

Next row (RS): Patt to m, sm, k2, p2tog, k6, p2tog, k2, sm, patt to m, sm, k13 (13, 13, 15, 15, 15, 15), sm, patt to m, sm, k2, p2tog, k6, p2tog, k2, sm, patt to end. 53 (61, 61, 63, 71, 71, 71) sts

Work 4 rows in moss st.
Cast off in moss.

SLEEVES (WORK BOTH ALIKE)

With RS of armhole facing, with shoulder seam at top, count 8 (8, 9, 10, 11, 12, 14) rows down from shoulder seam anti-clockwise and place a locking stitch marker (this will be marker A – use a different colour to distinguish this marker). Count 8 (8, 9, 10, 11, 12, 14) rows down from shoulder seam clockwise and place a second locking stitch marker (marker B). Place two more locking stitch markers (C and D) at the bottom of the armhole between the top of the cast-off sts and the first armhole decrease row (on the smallest size this will be directly next to the sts held on scrap yarn as no additional cast off rows were worked).

Using 4mm short circular ndl, starting at marker A, pick up and k14 (14, 16, 18, 18, 20, 24) sts between marker A and marker B, pick up and k21 (21, 22, 21, 24, 26, 28) sts up to next marker, pick up and k0 (2, 2, 5, 5, 6, 7) sts from cast-off sts, pick up and k1 st between cast-off sts and underarm sts, place 3 (4, 4, 5, 6, 7, 7) sts held on scrap yarn onto a spare ndl and k across them, pm for beg of rnd, k across 3 (4, 4, 5, 6, 7, 7) sts, pick up and k1 st between underarm sts and cast-off sts, pick up and k0 (2, 2, 5, 5, 6, 7) sts from cast-on sts, pick up and k21 (21, 22, 21, 24, 26, 28) sts to marker A. *64 (70, 74, 82, 90, 100, 110) sts*

Note: When picking up sts along the sides of the armhole, it may appear that there are too few sts to pick up for the number of rows. Do not worry, but simply pick up the specified number of sts evenly along the edge: the ratio of picked up sts to rows is unusual but when the sleeve cap is worked it will not appear holey.

Work short row sleeve cap as foll but **do not** pick up wraps, just leave them in place:
Short row 1 (RS): K14 (14, 16, 18, 18, 20, 24), w&t.
Short row 2 (WS): P14 (14, 16, 18, 18, 20, 24), w&t.
Short row 3: K up to and including wrapped st, p1, w&t.
Short row 4: P up to and including wrapped st, k1, w&t.
Short rows 5-8: Rep short rows 3-4 twice more (markers A and B can be removed at this point).

Short row 9: K up to and including wrapped st, w&t.
Short row 10: P up to and including wrapped st, w&t.
Rep short rows 9-10 until 4 sts remain before markers C and D.

Next short row: K to wrapped st, ssk (working wrapped st and next st as the decrease), k1, turn. *63 (69, 73, 81, 89, 99, 109) sts*
Next short row: Sl 1, p to wrapped st, p2tog (working wrapped st and next st as the decrease), p1, turn. *62 (68, 72, 80, 88, 98, 108) sts*
Next short row: Sl1, k to 1 st before gap, ssk, k1, turn. *1 st dec*
Next short row: Sl1, p to 1 st before gap, p2tog, p1, turn. *1 st dec*
Rep last 2 short rows a further 0 (1, 1, 2, 2, 2, 2) times. *60 (64, 68, 74, 82, 92, 102) sts*

Next short row: Sl1, k to 1 st before gap, k2tog tbl, k to beg of rnd marker. *1 st dec*
Next short row: K to 1 st before gap, k2tog tbl, k to end of rnd. *1 st dec 58 (62, 66, 72, 80, 90, 100) sts*

This is the end of the sleeve cap.
The sleeve will now be worked in rnds – switch to DPNs as the st count reduces.

Knit 7 rnds.

Dec rnd: K2, ssk, k to 4 sts from m, k2tog, k2. *56 (60, 64, 70, 78, 88, 98) sts*

Knit 22 (15, 13, 9, 7, 5, 4) rnds.
Rep Dec rnd. *2 sts dec*
Rep last 23 (16, 14, 10, 8, 6, 5) rnds a further 3 (5, 6, 9, 11, 16, 20) times. *48 (48, 50, 50, 54, 54, 56) sts*

Work straight until sleeve measures 39.5 (40.5, 40.5, 42, 42, 43, 43)cm/15½ (16, 16, 16½, 16½, 17, 17)" from underarm.

Change to 3.75mm DPNs.
Rnd 1: *K1, p1; rep from * to end.
Rnd 2: *P1, k1; rep from * to end.

Rep these 2 rnds a further 3 times.
Cast off in rib.

FINISHING

Weave in ends and block to measurements. Block the fronts flat and note that they will naturally be shorter than back.

SCHEMATIC: FRONT VIEW

SCHEMATIC: BACK VIEW

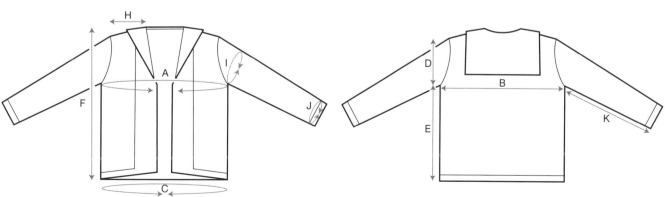

withernsea

by Alison Moreton

A tunic with cable straps and pocket detail, sized for adults and children (see page 43).

ADULT SIZES

PATTERN NOTES

Inspired by the traditional stitch pattern as recorded in ganseys from Withernsea and Patrington, the cable is worked in a 7-row repeat. By using this pattern as recorded, cable crosses are worked on both RS and WS rows. Although this is something I would usually try to avoid as a knitter and designer, I wanted to keep this link with the original stitch pattern. If you don't like doing cable crosses on the WS, we suggest crossing the cable every 8th row – if you want to use this option, then use it for the whole garment beginning at the bottom of the bodice.

ADULT SIZING

XS (S, M, L, XL, 2XL, 3XL) (see sizing table for more info)

YARN USED

baa ram ewe Dovestone DK in shade:
Bishopthorpe, 4 (4, 5, 5, 6, 6, 7) x 100g skeins

GAUGE

22 sts x 30 rows = 10cm/4" blocked and measured over stocking stitch on 4mm (US 6) needles
24 sts x 34 rnds = 10cm/4" blocked and measured over ladder stitch pattern worked flat and in the rnd on 3.75mm (US 5) needles

NEEDLES USED

3.75mm (US 5) circular needle 80cm/32" or longer for larger sizes – for XS size, you may wish to use a 3.75mm (US 5), 60cm/24" length for the bodice.
4mm (US 6) circular needle 80cm/32" or longer for larger sizes
Additional 3.75mm (US 5) **and** 3.25mm (US 3) needles of any type

SIZING TABLE: ADULTS

	xs	s	m	l	xl	2xl	3xl	
TO FIT BUST								
	71-76	81-86	91.5-96.5	101.5-106.5	111.5-117	122-127	132-137	cm
	28-30	32-34	36-38	40-42	44-46	48-50	52-54	in
CROSS BACK - A ON SCHEMATIC								
	37	38	42	44.5	44.5	46	46	cm
	14½	15	16½	17½	17½	18	18	in
FINISHED BUST - B ON SCHEMATIC								
	79	89	99	109	119	129.5	140	cm
	31	35	39	43	47	51	55	in
UNDERBUST - C ON SCHEMATIC								
	73.5	84	94	104	114	124.5	134.5	cm
	29	33	37	41	45	49	53	in
CIRCUMFERENCE AT BOTTOM - D ON SCHEMATIC								
	99	106.5	117	127	137	150	160	cm
	39	42	46	50	54	59	63	in
ARMHOLE DEPTH - E ON SCHEMATIC								
	19	20.5	21.5	23	24	25.5	26.5	cm
	7½	8	8½	9	9½	10	10½	in
UNDERARM TO BOTTOM OF BODICE - F ON SCHEMATIC								
	11.5	11.5	12.5	12.5	14	14	15	cm
	4½	4½	5	5	5½	5½	6	in
BACK NECK TO BOTTOM OF BODICE - G ON SCHEMATIC								
	30.5	31.5	24	25.5	8	39	42	cm
	12	12½	13½	14	15	15½	16½	in
UNDERARM TO HEM - H ON SCHEMATIC								
	55.5	55.5	55.5	55.5	55.5	55.5	55.5	cm
	22	22	22	22	22	22	22	in
BOTTOM OF BODICE TO HEM - I ON SCHEMATIC								
	44.5	44.5	43	43	42	42	40.5	cm
	17½	17½	17	17	16½	16½	16	in
FULL LENGTH - J ON SCHEMATIC								
	74.5	76	77	78.5	79.5	81	82.5	cm
	29½	30	30½	31	31½	32	32½	in

OTHER SUPPLIES

Stitch markers; Locking stitch markers; Cable needle; Smooth scrap yarn in a contrasting colour for provisional cast-ons; Crochet hook in a similar size to needles for provisional cast-ons; Ruler

ABBREVIATIONS

A list of standard abbreviations appears on page 72 and also on both cover flaps.

ABBREVIATIONS USED IN PATTERN

CABLES
C6F
Worked on RS: Sl 3 sts to cn and hold in front, k3, k3 from cn
Worked on WS: Sl 3 sts to cn and hold in front, p3, p3 from cn

CHARTS: WRITTEN INSTRUCTIONS

LADDER PATTERN, WORKED IN THE ROUND

Rnds 1-2: Knit.
Rnd 3: Purl.
Rnds 4-7: Knit.

LADDER PATTERN, WORKED FLAT

Row 1 (RS): Knit.
Row 2 (WS): Purl.
Rows 3-4: Purl.
Row 5: Knit.
Row 6: Purl.
Row 7: Knit.
Row 8: Purl.
Rows 9-11: Knit.
Row 12: Purl.
Row 13: Knit.
Row 14: Purl.

BASKET PATTERN, WORKED IN THE ROUND

Rnds 1-2: *P2, k2; rep from * to end.
Rnds 3-4: *K2, p2; rep from * to end.

BASKET PATTERN, WORKED FLAT

Row 1: P2, *k2, p2; rep from * to end.
Rows 2-3: K2, *p2, k2; rep from * to end.
Row 4: As for row 1.

CABLE PATTERN, WORKED IN THE ROUND

Rnds 1-2: P2, k6, p2.
Rnd 3: P2, C6F, p2.
Rnds 4-7: P2, C6F, p2.

CABLE PATTERN, WORKED FLAT

Row 1 (RS): P2, k6, p2.
Row 2 (WS): K2, p6, k2.
Row 3: P2, C6F, p2.
Row 4: Rep row 2.
Row 5: Rep row 1.
Rows 6-9: Rep rows 4-5.
Row 10: K2, C6F, k2.
Row 11: Rep row 1.
Row 12: Rep row 2.
Rows 13-14: Rep rows 11-12.

HINTS AND TIPS

When working the i-cord cast offs, pay close attention to the tension and ensure that it is neither too tight, causing the edges to draw in, nor too loose, causing the edges to flip or ruffle. If necessary, undo work and use a smaller needle size to knit the i-cord to tighten a loose edge or a larger needle size to loosen a tight edge.

After working a provisional cast on at the start of an I-cord edge, if the yarn is at the 'wrong' end of the 3 sts cast on, don't worry: you can take the yarn behind the stitches and begin working i-cord just as you would if working standalone i-cord.

If you need a longer tunic, work additional plain rounds between decrease rounds in the skirt. For a shorter tunic, omit some plain rounds evenly spaced between decrease rounds. Making a longer tunic will require more yarn.

SCHEMATIC

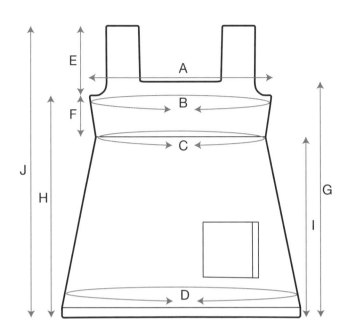

CHART: CABLE PATTERN, WORKED FLAT

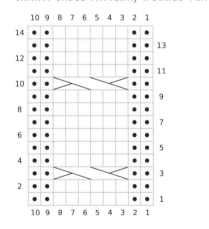

KEY

☐ RS: knit WS: purl

• RS: purl WS: knit

◇ C6F

CHART: CABLE PATTERN, WORKED IN THE ROUND

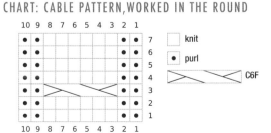

☐ knit

• purl

◇ C6F

WRITTEN INSTRUCTIONS: ADULT SIZES

SKIRT

Using 4mm ndl, cast on 216 (232, 252, 276, 296, 324, 348) sts. Join to work in the rnd, being careful not to twist and pm to indicate beg of rnd.

Rnds 1-2: *K2, p2; rep from * to end.
Rnds 3-4: *P2, k2; rep from * to end.
Rnds 5-6: Rep rnds 1-2.
Rnd 7: K108 (116, 126, 138, 148, 162, 174), pm for side seam, k to end.

Knit 7 rnds.

Work skirt shaping but please read the following section before continuing as you will be working two sets of instructions AT THE SAME TIME.

Knit 7 (7, 8, 7, 7, 6, 6) rnds.

Dec rnd: [K3, ssk, k to 5 sts before m, k2tog, k3, sm] twice. *4 sts dec*

Rep last 8 (8, 9, 8, 8, 7, 7) rnds a further 13 (12, 11, 12, 11, 13, 13) times. *160 (180, 204, 224, 248, 268, 292) sts*

AT THE SAME TIME when skirt measures 10cm/4" from cast-on edge, work foll pocket placement rnd: K20 (22, 24, 28, 30, 34, 36), p18, k to end.

Work straight until skirt measures 44.5 (44.5, 43, 43, 42, 42, 40.5)cm/17½ (17½, 17, 17, 16½, 16½, 16)" from cast-on edge.

BODICE
Change to 3.75mm ndl.
Rnd 1: Purl.
Rnd 2: Knit and inc 7 (8, 8, 9, 9, 11, 11) sts evenly **between each set** of markers. *14 (16, 18, 18, 18, 22, 22) sts inc; 174 (196, 220, 242, 266, 290, 314) sts*
Rnd 3: Purl.
Rnd 4: Knit and inc 8 (9, 9, 10, 10, 11, 11) sts evenly **between each set** of markers. *16 (18, 20, 20, 20, 22, 22) sts inc; 190 (214, 238, 262, 286, 312, 336) sts*

COMMENCE BODICE PATTERN
Rnd 1: *Work 5 (7, 11, 16, 22, 27, 33) sts in Ladders patt, pm, work 8 sts in Basket patt, p1, m1, k6, m1, p1, work 8 sts in Basket patt, pm, work 5 (7, 7, 8, 8, 9, 9) sts in Ladders patt, pm, p1, m1, k6, m1, p1, pm, work 11 (15, 19, 19, 19, 20, 20) sts in Ladders patt, pm, p1, m1, k6, m1, p1, pm, work 5 (7, 7, 8, 8, 9, 9) sts in Ladders patt, pm, work 8 sts in Basket patt, p1, m1, k6, m1, p1, work 8 sts in Basket patt, pm, work 5 (7, 11, 16, 22, 27, 33) sts in Ladders patt; rep from * once more. *16 sts inc, 206 (230, 254, 278, 302, 328, 352) sts*

Rnd 2: Working rnd 2 of each st patt, *work Ladders patt to m, sm, work 8 sts in Basket patt, work next 10 sts in Cable patt, work next 8 sts in Basket patt, sm, work Ladders patt to m, sm, work next 10 sts in Cable patt, sm, work Ladders patt to m, sm, work next 10 sts in Cable patt, sm, work Ladders patt to m, sm, work next 8 sts in Basket patt, work next 10 sts in Cable patt, work next 8 sts in Basket patt, sm, work Ladders pattern to m, sm; rep from * once more.

Working the next rnd of each stitch patt, continue as foll:
Rnd 3: M1, pm, patt to side seam m, m1, pm, patt to end. *208 (232, 256, 280, 304, 330, 354) sts*
Work 6 rnds straight in patt as set.

Inc rnd: M1, k to m, m1, patt to side seam m, sm, m1, k to m, m1, sm, patt to end. *4 sts inc*

Rep last 7 rnds twice more. *220 (244, 268, 292, 316, 342, 366) sts*

Work straight in patt as established until bodice measures 11.5 (11.5, 12.5, 12.5, 14, 14, 15) cm/4½ (4½, 5, 5, 5½, 5½, 6)" from first purl rnd.

SEPARATE FOR FRONT AND BACK
Row 1: Patt to 1 (3, 5, 6, 8, 9, 10) sts before second m, turn leaving rem 111 (125, 139, 152, 166, 180, 193) sts unworked. *109 (119, 129, 140, 150, 162, 173) sts*
Row 2 (WS): Work in patt, using charts/written instructions for flat knitting, taking care to begin on the correct row to continue patt as established, to 1 (3, 5, 6, 8, 9, 10) sts before beg of rnd marker, turn.

You will now work across these 101 (109, 117, 127, 135, 146, 156) sts for the Front.

**

SIZES L-3XL ONLY
Cast off – (–, –, 3, 3, 4, 5) sts at beg of next 2 rows, patt to end. *– (–, –, 121, 129, 138, 146) sts*

SIZES XL-3XL ONLY
Cast off – (–, –, –, 2, 3, 3) sts at beg of next 2 rows, patt to end. *– (–, –, –, 125, 132, 140) sts*

SIZE 3XL ONLY
Cast off – (–, –, –, –, –, 2) sts at beg of next 2 rows, patt to end. *– (–, –, – –, –, 136) sts*

ALL SIZES AGAIN
Row 1: K1, ssk, patt to 3 sts before end, k2tog, k1. *2 sts dec*
Row 2: Patt to end.
Rep rows 1-2 a further 5 (5, 7, 9, 11, 13, 15) times. *89 (97, 101, 103, 103, 106, 106) sts*

Break yarn.

Place first 24 sts on scrap yarn for shoulder strap, place next 41 (49, 53, 55, 55, 58, 58) sts onto spare 3.75mm ndl for neck, place rem 24 sts on scrap yarn for shoulder strap.

With RS of neck facing, using crochet chain provisional cast-on, cast 3 sts onto left ndl.

WORK I-CORD CAST OFF
Using 3.25mm ndl to knit with, [*k2, ssk, sl these 3 sts from right to left ndl; rep from * to m, rm] twice, *k2, sssk, sl these 3 sts from right to left ndl; rep from last * to next m, rm, *k2, ssk, sl these 3 sts from right to left ndl; rep from last * to next m, rm, *k2, sssk, sl these 3 sts from right to left ndl; rep from last * to next m, *k2, ssk, sl these 3 sts from right to left ndl; rep from last * until all neck sts have been worked and 3 sts rem. Sl these sts to a locking stitch marker leaving the yarn attached.

BACK
Return to 119 (135, 151, 165, 181, 196, 210) sts on original working ndl.

Place 9 (13, 17, 19, 23, 25, 27) sts from each end of ndl on scrap yarn for underarm.

With RS facing, rejoin a new ball of yarn and continue on 101 (109, 117, 127, 135, 146, 156) sts as folls:
Row 1 (RS): Patt to end, turn.

Row 2 (WS): Work across sts in patt using charts/written instructions for flat knitting, taking care to begin on the correct row to continue patt as established.

Work as for Front from ******.

RIGHT FRONT STRAP

Place 3 sts from end of i-cord cast off for neck onto 3.75mm ndl and knit them, place 24 sts held on scrap yarn for right front strap onto a spare ndl and patt across these sts, using crochet chain provisional method cast 3 sts onto the end of the ndl. *30 sts*

***

Straps will be worked with 3 st applied i-cord edges on each side as foll:
Next row (WS): Sl 3 sts pwise wyif, patt to last 3 sts, p3.
Next row (RS): Sl 3 sts pwise wyib, patt to last 3 sts, k3.

Continue in patt as set until strap measures 19 (20.5, 21.5, 23, 24, 25.5, 26.5)cm/7½ (8, 8½, 9, 9½, 10, 10½)" from underarm, finishing after row 6 OR row 13 of Cable patt. To measure straps accurately, lay a ruler on the work at the level of the underarm sts, ensuring that the ruler is parallel to the bottom of the bodice, and measure the strap length vertically from the ruler. Make a note of how many cable repeats were worked and work the same for each strap.

Work foll row to dec 1 st in each of the reverse St st columns (this ensures the cast off edge stays the same width) working either the next WS or RS depending on where in the cable repeat you finish:

Next row (WS): Sl 3 sts pwise, patt 4 sts, k2tog, p6, k2tog, patt to last 3 sts, p3.
OR
Next row (RS): Sl 3 sts pwise, patt 4 sts, p2tog, k6, p2tog, patt to last 3 sts, k3.

Place completed strap sts on scrap yarn.

LEFT BACK STRAP

Left back strap is worked in the same way as Right front strap.

LEFT FRONT STRAP

Using 3.75mm ndl and crochet chain provisional method, cast on 3 sts, place 24 sts held on scrap yarn for right front strap onto a spare ndl and patt across these sts, undo provisional cast-on at start of neck cast-off and place these 3 sts onto a spare ndl and knit across them.

Work as for right front strap from *******.

RIGHT BACK STRAP
Right back strap is worked the same way as left front strap.

JOIN SHOULDERS
Turn work inside out so that WS is facing. Place first and last 3 sts of each strap onto locking stitch markers or safety pins. Place 24 sts from centre of left front strap onto one point of 3.75mm ndl and place 24 sts from centre of left back strap onto the other point of the same ndl. Using the spare ndl, work a 3-needle cast off across all sts.

Repeat for right straps.

Place each pair of 3 sts from edges of straps onto ndls and graft together using Kitchener stitch – this gives a seamless finish to the i-cord borders. If you prefer, you can simply work a 3-needle cast off over all strap sts.

RIGHT UNDERARM
With WS facing, using 3.75mm ndl, pick up and p9 (9, 12, 15, 19, 22, 27) sts along armhole edge, place 9 (13, 17, 19, 23, 25, 27) sts onto left ndl and purl across them, pick up and p9 (9, 12, 15, 19, 22, 27) sts along armhole edge. Turn work.

Undo provisional cast-on from front right strap edge, place these 2 sts on left ndl and pick up 1 additional st.
Work i-cord cast off as foll: *K2, ssk, sl these 3 sts from right to left ndl; rep from * until all neck sts have been worked and 3 sts rem. Undo provisional cast-on from right back strap edge—there will be 2 sts from the cast-on. Pick up one additional st. Graft these sts together.

Work left underarm in the same way.

POCKET
Using 3.75mm ndl, cast on 38 sts.

Row 1 (RS): Work cable patt across 10 sts, pm, work 28 sts in Basket patt.

Row 2 (WS): Work Basket patt to m, sm, work cable patt over next 10 sts.
Rep rows 1-2 a further 21 times.

WORK I-CORD CAST OFF AS FOLLOWS
Using knitted on cast on method, cast 3 sts onto left ndl. *K2, sssk, sl these 3 sts from right to left ndl; rep from * to m, rm. All cable sts have been worked. By working sssk the cable sts are cast off without causing flaring of the cast-off edge.

Cast off rem sts as foll: *K2, ssk, sl these 3 sts from right to left ndl; rep from * until all pocket sts have been worked. Break yarn and thread through rem sts. Fasten off.

I-CORD HEM
Hold the tunic with RS facing, at the bottom cast-on edge.

Starting at the 'side seam' (beginning of rnd or midpoint of rnd), using a 3.75mm ndl, pick up and k162 (174, 189, 207, 222, 243, 261) sts (3 sts picked up for every 4 sts cast on). Break yarn.

Cast 3 sts onto left ndl using knitted on cast on. *K2, ssk, sl 3 sts from right to left ndl; rep from * until all sts picked up have been used up. Cast off rem 3 sts. Join beg and end of i-cord with a small seam.

You may find it easier to work the i-cord using a 3.75mm DPN as the right ndl tip. As you go, check that the hem lays flat, without being tugged in. If this is happening, knit the i-cord more loosely using a larger DPN. If this does not solve the problem, then you will need to work the picking up round again, this time picking up more sts.

FINISHING
Weave in and block tunic and pocket separately.
Sew pocket to left front of tunic, lining up the bottom of the pocket with the purl sts created in the pocket placement rnd.

withernsea

CHILDREN'S SIZES

SIZING
To fit age: 2 (4, 6, 8, 10) years (see sizing table for more info)

YARN USED
baa ram ewe Dovestone DK in shade:
Rhubarb, 2 (2, 3, 3, 4) x 100g skeins

GAUGE
22 sts x 30 rows = 10cm/4" blocked and measured over stocking stitch on 4mm (US 6) needles
24 sts x 34 rnds = 10cm/4" blocked and measured over ladder stitch pattern worked flat and in the rnd on 3.75mm (US 5) needles

NEEDLES USED
3.75mm (US 5) circular needle 60cm/24" length
4mm (US 6) circular needle 60cm/24" length – for smallest size you may wish to use a 3.75mm (US 5), 40cm/16" length for the bodice.
Additional 3.75mm (US 5) **and** 3.25mm (US 3) needles of any type

SIZING TABLE: CHILDREN

AGE					
2	**4**	**6**	**8**	**10**	
TO FIT CHEST					
53.5	58.5	63.5	67.5	71	cm
21	23	25	26½	28	in
CROSS BACK - A ON SCHEMATIC					
23.5	25	26	27.5	28.5	cm
9¼	9¾	10¼	10¾	11¼	in
FINISHED CHEST - B ON SCHEMATIC					
58.5	63.5	68.5	72.5	76	cm
23	25	27	28½	30	in
CIRCUMFERENCE AT BOTTOM - D ON SCHEMATIC					
71	75	79	86.5	90	cm
28	29½	31	34	35½	in
ARMHOLE DEPTH - E ON SCHEMATIC					
13.5	14.6	15	16.5	18	cm
5¼	5¾	6	6½	7	in
FULL LENGTH - J ON SCHEMATIC					
39.5	46	53.5	61	66	cm
15½	18	21	24	26	in
UNDERARM TO BOTTOM OF BODICE - F ON SCHEMATIC					
5	6.5	7.5	9	10	cm
2	2½	3	3½	4	in
BACK NECK TO BOTTOM OF BODICE - G ON SCHEMATIC					
16	18.5	20.5	23	25.5	cm
6¼	7¼	8	9	10	in
UNDERARM TO HEM - H ON SCHEMATIC					
28.5	33.5	40.5	47	51	cm
11¼	13¼	16	18½	20	in
BOTTOM OF BODICE TO HEM - I ON SCHEMATIC					
23.5	27.5	33	38	10.5	cm
9¼	10¾	13	15	16	in

SCHEMATIC

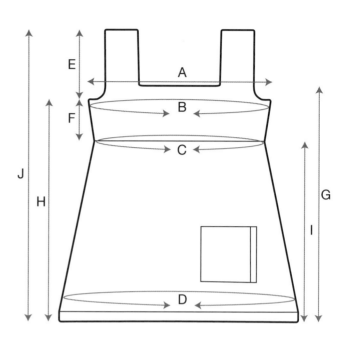

CHART: CABLE PATTERN, WORKED FLAT

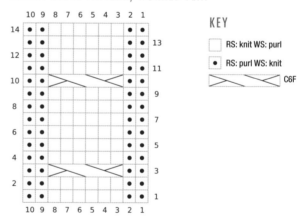

KEY

☐ RS: knit WS: purl

● RS: purl WS: knit

⬓ C6F

CHART: CABLE PATTERN, WORKED IN THE ROUND

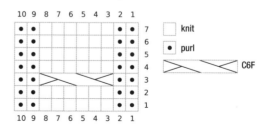

☐ knit

● purl

⬓ C6F

WRITTEN INSTRUCTIONS: CHILDREN'S SIZES

SKIRT

Using 4mm ndl, cast on 156 (164, 172, 188, 196) sts. Join to work in the rnd, being careful not to twist and pm to indicate beg of rnd.

Rnds 1-2: *K2, p2; rep from * to end.
Rnds 3-4: *P2, k2; rep from * to end.
Rnds 5-6: Rep rnds 1-2.
Rnd 7: K78 (82, 86, 94, 98), pm for side seam, k to end.

Knit 7 rnds.

Work skirt shaping but please read the following section before continuing as you will be working two sets of instructions AT THE SAME TIME.

Knit 5 (7, 10, 10, 12) rnds.

Dec rnd: [K3, ssk, k to 5 sts before m, k2tog, k3, sm] twice. *4 sts dec*

Rep last 6 (8, 11, 11, 13) rnds a further 6 (5, 5, 6, 6) times. *128 (140, 148, 160, 168) sts*

AT THE SAME TIME, when skirt measures 5 (5, 7.5, 7.5, 7.5)cm/2 (2, 3, 3, 3)" from cast-on edge, work foll pocket placement rnd: K14 (15, 16, 16, 17), p15, k to end.

Work straight until skirt measures 23.5 (27.5, 33, 38, 40.5)cm/ 9¼ (10¾, 13, 15, 16)" from cast-on edge.

BODICE

Change to 3.75mm ndl.

Rnd 1: Purl.
Rnd 2: Knit and inc 5 sts evenly **between each set** of markers. *10 sts inc; 138 (150, 158, 170, 178) sts*
Rnd 3: Purl.

Rnd 4: Knit and inc 4 (4, 6, 5, 5) sts evenly **between each set** of markers. *8 (8, 12, 10, 10) sts inc; 146 (158, 170, 180, 188) sts*

COMMENCE BODICE PATTERN

Rnd 1: *Work 6 (7, 10, 12, 13) sts in Ladders patt, pm, work next 6 sts in Basket patt, p1, m1, k6, m1, p1, work next 6 sts in Basket patt, pm, work 21 (25, 25, 26, 28) sts in Ladders patt, pm, work next 6 sts in Basket patt, p1, m1, k6, m1, p1, work next 6 sts in Basket pattern, pm, work next 6 (7, 10, 12, 13) sts in Ladders pattern; rep from * once more. *8 sts inc; 154 (166, 178, 188, 196) sts*

Rnd 2: Working rnd 2 of each st patt, *work Ladders patt to m, sm, work 6 sts in Basket patt, work 10 sts in Cable patt, work 6 sts in Basket patt, sm, work Ladders patt to m, sm, work next 6 sts in Basket patt, work next 10 sts in Cable patt, work next 6 sts in Basket patt, sm, work in Ladders patt to m, sm; rep from * once more.

Working the next rnd of each stitch patt, work straight until bodice measures 5 (6.5, 7.5, 9, 10)cm/2 (2½, 3, 3½, 4)" from first purl rnd.

SEPARATE FOR FRONT AND BACK

FRONT

Row 1: Patt to 4 (5, 7, 8, 9) sts before side seam m, turn leaving rem sts unworked.

Row 2: Work in patt, using charts/written instructions for flat knitting, taking care to begin on the correct row to continue patt as established, to 4 (5, 7, 8, 9) sts before beg of rnd m, turn. *69 (73, 75, 78, 80) sts*

Row 3: K1, ssk, work in patt to 3 sts before end, k2tog, k1. *2 sts dec*
Row 4: Patt to end.
Rep rows 3-4 a further 3 (3, 4, 5, 5) times. *61 (65, 65, 66, 68) sts*
Break yarn.

Place first 18 sts on scrap yarn for shoulder strap, place next 25 (29, 29, 30, 32) sts on spare 3.75mm ndl for neck, place rem 18 sts on scrap yarn for shoulder strap.

With RS of neck facing, using crochet chain provisional cast-on, cast 3 sts onto left ndl.

WORK I-CORD CAST OFF
Using 3.25mm ndl to knit with, *k2, ssk, sl these 3 sts from right to left ndl; rep from * until all neck sts have been worked and 3 sts rem. Sl these sts to a locking stitch marker leaving the yarn attached.

BACK
Return to 85 (93, 103, 110, 116) sts rem on original ndl.

Place 8 (10, 14, 16, 18) sts from each end of ndl on scrap yarn for underarm. *69 (73, 75, 78, 80) sts*

With RS facing, rejoin a new ball of yarn and continue as folls:
Row 1 (RS): Patt to end, turn.
Row 2 (WS): Work across sts in patt using charts/written instructions for flat knitting, taking care to begin on the correct row to continue patt as established.

Work as for Front beg with Row 3.

RIGHT FRONT STRAP
Place 3 sts from end of i-cord cast off for neck onto 3.75mm ndl and knit them, place 18 sts held on scrap yarn for right front strap onto a spare ndl and patt across these sts in patt, using crochet chain provisional method cast 3 sts onto the end of the ndl. *24 sts*

**
Straps will be worked with 3 st applied i-cord edges on each side as foll:
Next row (WS): Sl 3 sts pwise wyif, patt to last 3 sts, p3.
Next row (RS): Sl 3 sts pwise wyib, patt to last 3 sts, k3.

Continue in patt as set until strap measures 13.5 (14.5, 15, 16.5, 18)cm/5¼ (5¾, 6, 6½, 7)" from underarm, finishing after row 6 OR row 13 of Cable patt. To measure straps accurately, lay a ruler on the work at the level of the underarm sts, ensuring that the ruler is parallel to the bottom of the bodice, and measure the strap length vertically from the ruler. Make a note of how many cable repeats were worked and work the same for each strap.

Work foll row to dec 1 st in each of the reverse St st columns (this ensures the cast off edge stays the same width) working either the next WS or RS depending on where in the cable repeat you finish:

Next row (WS): Sl 3 sts pwise, patt 4 sts, k2tog, p6, k2tog, patt to last 3 sts, p3.
OR
Next row (RS): Sl 3 sts pwise, patt 4 sts, p2tog, k6, p2tog, patt to last 3 sts, k3.

Place completed strap sts on scrap yarn.

LEFT BACK STRAP
Left back strap is worked in the same way as Right front strap.

LEFT FRONT STRAP
Using 3.75mm ndl and crochet chain provisional method, cast on 3 sts, place 18 sts held on scrap yarn for right front strap onto a spare ndl and patt across these sts, undo provisional cast-on at start of neck cast-off and place these 3 sts onto a spare ndl and knit across them.

Work as for right front strap from **.

RIGHT BACK STRAP
Right back strap is worked the same way as Left front strap.

JOIN SHOULDERS
Turn work inside out so that WS is facing. Place first and last 3 sts of each strap onto locking stitch markers or safety pins. Place 18 sts from centre of left front strap onto one point of 3.75mm ndl and place 18 sts from centre of left back strap onto the other point of the same circular ndl. Using the spare ndl, work a 3-needle cast off across all sts.

Repeat for right straps.

Place each pair of 3 sts from edges of straps onto ndls and graft together using Kitchener stitch – this gives a seamless finish to the i-cord borders. If you prefer, you can simply work a 3-needle cast off over all strap sts.

RIGHT UNDERARM
With WS facing, using 3.75mm ndl, pick up and p6 (6, 8, 9, 9) sts along armhole edge, place 8 (10, 14, 16, 18) sts onto left ndl and purl across them, pick up and p6 (6, 8, 9, 9) sts along armhole edge. Turn work.

Undo provisional cast-on from front right strap edge, place these 2 sts on left ndl and pick up 1 additional st.

Work i-cord cast off as foll: *K2, ssk, sl these 3 sts from right to left ndl; rep from * until all neck sts have been worked and 3 sts rem. Undo provisional cast-on from right back strap edge – there will be 2 sts from the cast-on. Pick up one additional st. Graft these sts together.

Work left underarm in the same way.

POCKET
Using 3.75mm ndl, cast on 30 sts.

Row 1 (RS): Work cable patt across 10 sts, pm, work 20 sts in Basket patt.
Row 2 (WS): Work Basket patt to m, sm, work cable patt over next 10 sts.
Rep rows 1-2 a further 10 times.

WORK I-CORD CAST OFF AS FOLL
Using knitted on cast on method, cast 3 sts onto left ndl. *K2, sssk, sl these 3 sts from right to left ndl; rep from * to m, rm. All cable sts have been worked. By working sssk the cable sts are cast off without causing flaring of the cast off edge.

Cast off rem sts as foll: *K2, ssk, slip these 3 sts from right to left ndl; rep from * until all pocket sts have been worked. Break yarn and thread through rem sts. Fasten off.

I-CORD HEM
Hold the tunic with RS facing, at the bottom cast-on edge.

Starting at the 'side seam' (beginning of round or midpoint of round), using a 3.75mm circular ndl, pick up and k117 (123, 129, 141, 147) sts (3 sts picked up for every 4 sts cast on). Break yarn.

Cast 3 sts onto left ndl using knitted on cast on. *K2, ssk, sl 3 sts from right to left ndl; rep from * until all sts picked up have been used up. Cast off rem 3 sts. Join beg and end of i-cord with a small seam.
Note: You could cast on the 3 sts using a provisional cast on and then graft at the end, but because the side of the hem is not especially visible the extra work is probably not worth it.

You may find it easier to work the i-cord using a 3.75mm DPN as the right ndl tip. As you go, check that the hem lays flat, without being tugged in. If this is happening, knit the i-cord more loosely using a larger DPN. If this does not solve the problem, then you will need to work the picking up round again, this time picking up more sts.

FINISHING
Weave in and block tunic and pocket separately.
Sew pocket to left front of tunic, lining up the bottom of the pocket with the purl sts created in the pocket placement rnd.

robin hood's bay

by Graeme Knowles-Miller

This saddle shoulder jumper is a modern take on a classic gansey with the moss and cable pattern taken from the easily-recognised Robin Hood's Bay pattern. Short-row shoulder caps are a contemporary addition to the historical in-the-round style construction.

YARN USED
baa ram ewe Dovestone DK in shade:
Bramley Baths, 4 (4, 5, 5, 6) x 100g skeins

SIZING
XS (S, M, L, XL, 2XL, 3XL) (see sizing table for more info)

GAUGE
22 sts x 30 rows = 10cm/4" blocked and measured over stocking stitch on 4mm (US 6) needles

NEEDLES USED
3.5mm (US 4) circular needle, 80cm/32" length
4mm (US 6) circular needle, 80cm/32" length
3.5mm (US 4) DPNs for sleeves
4mm (US 6) DPNs for sleeves

OTHER SUPPLIES
Stitch markers; Stitch holders or scrap yarn

SPECIAL INSTRUCTIONS
MOSS STITCH
Choosing either k1 or p1 to start alternate between k1 and p1 for the stated number of stitches. After turning and working back to these sts, work the same st as was worked on the previous round. ie (RS) P1, k1, p1, k1, p1 then work to end, (WS) work to last p st on previous row, p1, k1, p1, k1, p1.

CABLES
C6B on a RS row: Slip 3 sts to cn, hold in back, k3, k3 from cn.
C6B on a WS row: Slip 3 sts to cn, hold in back, p3, p3 from cn.

ABBREVIATIONS
A list of standard abbreviations appears on page 72 and also on both cover flaps.

HINTS AND TIPS
WRAP & TURN (W&T)
After a knit stitch: Bring the yarn to the front between the needles. Slip the next stitch pwise. Take the yarn to the back between the needles. Slip stitch back to left needle. Turn.
After a purl stitch: Bring the yarn to the back between the needles. Slip the next stitch pwise. Take the yarn to the front between the needles. Slip stitch back to right needle. Turn.
To pick up a wrap on a knit stitch: Use right needle to pick up the wrap from the front to the back, then put needle into the stitch knitwise, knit wrap and stitch together.
To pick up a wrap on a purl stitch: Use the right needle to pick up the wrap from the back to the front and place it on the left needle. Purl the wrap and the stitch together.

SIZING TABLE

	xs	s	m	l	xl	
TO FIT CHEST						
	86-91.5	96.5-101.5	106.5-111.5	116.5-122	127-132	cm
	34-36	38-40	42-44	46-48	50-52	in
ACTUAL CHEST – A ON SCHEMATIC						
	89	99	109	119	129	cm
	35	39	43	46¾	50¾	in
UNDERARM TO BOTTOM EDGE – B ON SCHEMATIC						
	40.5	42	44.5	45	46.5	cm
	16	16½	17½	17¾	18¼	in
SHOULDER WIDTH – C ON SCHEMATIC						
	40	42	45	46	47.5	cm
	15¾	16½	17¾	18	18¾	in
UPPER ARM – D ON SCHEMATIC						
	30.5	33	38	40.5	43	cm
	12	13	15	16	17	in
SLEEVE LENGTH – E ON SCHEMATIC						
	45.5	47	49.5	51	52	cm
	18	18½	19½	20	20½	in

Apologies.

There are some errors in this pattern.
Check out the inside back cover for
all the corrections.

WRITTEN INSTRUCTIONS

SADDLE SHOULDERS (MAKE 2 ALIKE)
Using 4mm ndl, cast on 14 (14, 17, 17, 19) sts. Do not join.
Row 1 (RS): Knit.
Row 2 (WS): K1, p to last st, k1.
Rep rows 1-2 until saddle measures 11 (11.5, 12.5, 12.5, 13) cm/4¼ (4½, 4¾, 5, 5¼)" from cast-on edge.
Place sts on holder.

BACK
With RS facing, pick up and k24 (25, 27, 27, 28) sts along saddle beg from live sts working to cast-on edge, cable cast on 38 (42, 44, 45, 46) sts for neck, with RS facing pick up and k24 (25, 27, 27, 28) sts from other saddle but this time beg at cast-on edge working towards live sts. *86 (92, 98, 99, 102) sts*
Next row (WS): K1, p to last st, k1.

Work short rows to shape the shoulders as foll:
Short row 1 (RS): K67 (72, 78, 79, 81), w&t
Short row 2 (WS): P51 (54, 58, 59, 60), w&t.
Short row 3: K57 (61, 65, 66, 67), w&t.
Short row 4: P63 (68, 72, 73, 74), w&t.
Short row 5: K69 (75, 79, 80, 81), w&t.
Short row 6: P76 (82, 86, 87, 88), w&t.
Short row 7: K to end, picking up and working the wraps with their st as you pass them.
Next row: K1, p to last st picking up and working the wraps with their st as you pass them, k1.

Work straight as foll:
Row 1 (RS): Knit.
Row 2 (WS): K1, p to last st, k1.

Rep rows 1-2 until back measures 17 (16, 15.5, 15, 13.5)cm/6¾ (6¼, 6, 6, 5¼)" from arm selvedge of picked-up sts at saddle, ending with a WS row.

SHAPE ARMHOLE
Continue in patt as set and working the increase one st in from each side, inc 1 st at each end of next row and then foll 3rd (3rd, 3rd, 2nd, 2nd) row 1 (3, 4, 9, 12) times ending with a WS row. *90 (100, 108, 119, 128) sts*

Place sts on scrap yarn or holder.

LEFT FRONT
With RS facing, working on left-hand side of neck, pick up and k24 (25, 27, 27, 28) sts along saddle beg at cast-on edge working towards live sts.
Next row (WS): K1, p to last 9 sts, k1, p6, k2.

Work incs and short rows to shape shoulders as foll, picking up and working the wraps with their st as you pass them:
Short row 1 (RS): K1, m1r, p1, k5 (5, 6, 6, 6), w&t. *25 (26, 28, 28, 29) sts*
Short row 2 (WS): P5 (5, 6, 6, 6), k to end.
Short row 3: K1, m1r, k1, p1, k6, p1, moss 5 (6, 7, 7, 8) *(Moss - see special instructions)*, w&t. *26 (27, 29, 29, 30) sts*
Short row 4: Moss 5 (6, 7, 7, 8), k1, p6, k2, p1, k1.

SCHEMATIC

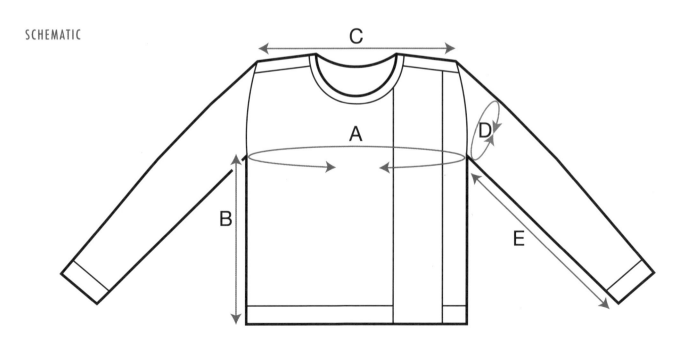

Short row 5: K1, m1r, p1, k1, p1, k6, p1, moss 8, k5 (6, 8, 8, 9), w&t. *27 (28, 30, 30, 31) sts*
Short row 6: P5 (6, 8, 8, 9), moss 8, k1, p6, k2, p1, k2.

Work in full rows again as foll:
Row 1 (RS): K1, m1r, k1, p1, k1, p1, k6, p1, moss 8, k to end picking up and working wraps with their st as you pass them. *28 (29, 31, 31, 32) sts*
Row 2 (WS) K1, patt to last st, k1.
Row 3: K1, m1r, moss to purl ridge st, p1, C6B, p1, moss 8, k to end. *29 (30, 32, 32, 33) sts*
Continue to inc 1 st at neck edge on RS rows to 39 (42, 44, 45, 47) sts, ending with a WS row and **AT THE SAME TIME** work a cable every 7th row - this will mean cabling occurs on alternate RS and WS rows. There will be 1 purl column and 8 moss sts each side of the cable.
Place sts on holder.

RIGHT FRONT
With RS facing, working on right-hand side of neck, pick up and k24 (25, 27, 27, 28) sts along saddle beg at live sts and working towards the cast-on sts.

Work incs and short rows to shape the shoulders as foll, picking up and working the wraps with their st as you pass them:
Short row 1 (WS): K1, m1p, p6 (6, 7, 7, 7), w&t. *25 (26, 28, 28, 29) sts*
Short rows 2, 4 & 6 (RS): K to end.
Short row 3: K1, m1p, p15 (16, 17, 17, 18), w&t. *26 (27, 29, 29, 30) sts*
Short row 5: K1, m1p, p22 (23, 25, 25, 26), w&t. *27 (28, 30, 30, 31) sts*

WORK IN FULL ROWS AGAIN
All foll WS rows: K1, m1p, p to end picking up and working wraps with their st as you pass them on the first row, k1. *1 st inc*
All foll RS rows: K to end.

Continue to inc 1 st at neck edge on WS rows to 39 (42, 44, 45, 47) sts, taking the inc sts into moss then St st patt, ending with a WS row.

With RS facing, join the two front pieces as foll:
K to end keeping moss and cable correct patt correct, cast on 8 (8, 10, 9, 8) sts, k across 39 (42, 44, 45, 47) sts left front sts. *86 (92, 98, 99, 102) sts*
Now work straight as foll:
Row 1 (WS): K1, p to last st, k1.
Row 2 (RS): Knit.
Rep rows 1-2 until front measures 17 (16, 15.5, 15, 13.5)cm/6¾ (6¼, 6, 6, 5¼)" from arm selvedge of picked-up sts at saddle, ending with a WS row.

SHAPE ARMHOLE
Continue in patt as set and working the increase one st in from each side, inc 1 st at each end of next row and then foll 3rd (3rd, 3rd, 2nd, 2nd) row 1 (3, 4, 9, 12) times ending with a WS row. *90 (100, 108, 119, 128) sts*

With RS facing, join the front and back pieces as foll:
Keeping moss and cable patt correct, work across front sts, cast on 6 (7, 9, 10, 12) sts for underarm, k across back sts, cast on 6 (7, 9, 10, 12) sts. *192 (214, 234, 258, 280) sts*
From this point onwards the body is worked in the rnd.

BODY
Continue in St st keeping the cable and moss patt down left front correct (cables still made every 7th row), until body measures 35.5 (37, 38, 39.5, 40.5)/14 (14½, 15, 15½, 16)" from underarm cast-on.
Next rnd: Work to moss sts, moss 8, p1, dec 1, k4, dec 1, p1, work to end of rnd. *190 (212, 232, 256, 278) sts*

SIZES 1 & 5 ONLY
Next rnd: Work 1 rnd decreasing 2 sts at sides. *188 (-, -, -, 276) sts*

Change to 3.5mm ndl.
Rib rnd: *K2, p2; rep from * to end.
Rep Rib rnd until rib measures 5cm/2".
Cast off loosely in rib.

SLEEVES

With RS of saddle facing, using 4mm ndl, join yarn at left side of saddle (when facing) and knit from stitch holder as foll: K1 (3, 2, 4, 4), k2tog, k3 (4, 4, 5, 3), k2tog, k3 (3, 3, 4, 3), [k2tog] 1 (0, 1, 0, 1) times, k1 (0, 2, 0, 3), pm (this will be mB), pick up and k30 (32, 32, 34, 35) sts down side of armhole to underarm cast-on point (approximately 1 st every 2 rows), pm (mC), pick up and k12 (14, 18, 20, 24) sts from underarm cast-on, pm (mD), pick up and k30 (32, 32, 34, 35) sts from other side of armhole to point at which yarn was joined, pm (mA). *83 (90, 96, 103, 110) sts*

Shape upper sleeve cap with short rows as foll:

Short row 1 (RS): Slip mA, k to 1 st after mB, w&t.
Short row 2 (WS): P to mA, w&t first st after mA.
Short row 3: K to wrapped st, k wrapped st with its wrap, sl 1 wyif, take yarn back, w&t.
Short row 4: P to wrapped st, purl wrapped st with its wrap, sl 1 wyib, bring yarn to front, w&t.
Rep short rows 3-4 twice more – this skips 1 st between each w&t easing the top of the shoulder cap into the side section.

Shape middle sleeve cap with short rows as foll:

Next short row (RS): K to wrapped st, k wrapped st with its wrap, w&t.
Next short row (WS): P to wrapped st, p wrapped st with its wrap, w&t.
Rep last 2 short rows, working back and forth across sleeve cap until 6 (7, 4, 5, 6) sts rem before mC and mD.

Shape lower sleeve cap with short rows as foll:

Note: The decrease will be made up of the wrapped st and the next st to be worked.
Next short row (RS)(Dec): K to wrapped st, k2tog with next st, w&t. *1 st dec*
Next short row (WS): P to wrapped st, p2tog with the next st, w&t. *1 st dec*
Rep last 2 short rows a further 4 (5, 3, 3, 4) times. *73 (78, 88, 96, 100) sts*

Next row (RS): Removing mC and mD as you pass them, k to wrapped st and work k2tog with next st 0 (0, 0, 1, 0) time, k5 (5, 6, 5, 6), pm. *73 (78, 88, 95, 100) sts*

Continue straight as foll:
Change to DPNs or preferred method for working small circumferences in the rnd.
Rnd 1: K3 (3, 4, 5, 6), k2tog with remaining wrapped st, k to end of rnd removing mA and mB when reached. *72 (77, 88, 94, 99) sts*
Rnd 2: Knit.
Next rnd (Dec): K1, ssk, k to last 3 sts, k2tog, k1. *2 sts dec*
Working St st in the rnd (knit every rnd), rep Dec rnd every 9th (8th, 7th, 6th, 6th) rnd 7 (15, 10, 22, 12) times, then following 8th (–, 6th, –, 5th) rnd 7 (–, 10, –, 12) times. *44 (47, 48, 50, 51) sts*

Work straight until sleeve measures 40.5 (42, 44.5, 45, 46)cm/16 (16½, 17½, 17¾, 18¼)" from underarm or 5cm/2" less than desired length.

Change to 3.5mm DPNs or preferred method for working small circumferences in the rnd.
Rib rnd: *K2, p2; rep from * to end and AT THE SAME TIME evenly decrease 0 (3, 0, 2, 3) sts across the rnd.
Rep Rib rnd without decreasing until rib measures 5cm/2".
Cast off in rib.

NECKBAND

With RS facing, using 3.5mm ndl pick up and k30 (32, 34, 36, 38) sts from neck left edge (1 st every row), 8 (8, 10, 9, 8) sts from centre neck, 30 (32, 34, 36, 38) sts from neck edge right (1 st every row), 11 (11, 13, 13, 14) sts across saddle, 29 (30, 33, 34, 35) sts across back (approximately 3 sts in 4) and 11 (11, 13, 13, 14) sts across saddle. *119 (124, 137, 141, 147) sts*

Row 1: *K2, p2; rep from * to end and AT THE SAME TIME evenly dec 7 (4, 5, 5, 7) sts across the rnd. *112 (120, 132, 136, 140) sts*

Work in 2x2 rib as set for 2.5cm / 1".
Cast off in rib.

FINISHING

Graft underarms using Kitchener Stitch
Weave in ends and block to shape measurements.

sandsend

by Alison Moreton and Graeme Knowles-Miller

A patchwork blanket with a sampler effect, using a variety of the stitch patterns found throughout this book.

PATTERN NOTES
Construction in strips means sewing up is just three straight seams.

YARN USED
baa ram ewe Dovestone DK in shades:
Rhubarb, 2 x 100g skeins
Bishopthorpe, 2 x 100g skeins
Viking, 2 x 100g skeins

GAUGE
22 sts x 30 rows = 10cm/4" blocked and measured over stocking stitch on 4mm (US 6) needles

NEEDLES USED
4mm (US 6) knitting needles

OTHER SUPPLIES
Cable needle

SIZING
One size: 88 x 132cm/34½ x 52"

SPECIAL INSTRUCTIONS
The Sandsend blanket is made in four strips. Each strip is worked in blocks.
We recommend that you make the first block of strip 1, block and measure it, and if you match the specified tension, proceed with the rest of the blanket. If your tension varies then adjust the needle size and swatch again.
If you count the number of rows worked in block 1, you can then ensure that each block is worked with the same number of rows (and the half-blocks at the beginning and end of strips 2 and 4 are worked with half that number of rows). This will make it easier to sew up the blanket.

CABLE
C6B: Slip 3 sts to cn and hold in back, k3, k3 from cn.

ABBREVIATIONS
A list of standard abbreviations appears on page 72 and also on both cover flaps.

CHARTS: WRITTEN INSTRUCTIONS

BLOCK 1: WITHERNSEA
Rows 1-3: Knit.
Row 4 (WS): K16, m1p, k4, m1p, k26. *48 sts*
Row 5 (RS): K24, p2, k6, [p2, k2] 4 times.
Row 6: K4, [p2, k2] 3 times, p6, k2, p22, k2.
Row 7: K2, p24, C6B, p4, [k2, p2] twice, k4.
Row 8: [K2, p2] 3 times, k4, p6, k2, p22, k2.
Row 9: Rep row 5.
Row 10: Rep row 6.
Row 11: K24, p2, k6, p4, [k2, p2] twice, k4.
Row 12: Rep row 8.
Row 13: K2, p24, C6B, [p2, k2] 4 times.
Row 14: Rep row 6.
Row 15: Rep row 11.
Row 16: Rep row 8.
Rep rows 5-16 until block measures length specified in the Written Instructions on p57, ending with a WS row.
Next row: K26, k2tog, k4, k2tog, k16. *46 sts*
Next 3 rows: Knit.

BLOCK 2: FLAMBOROUGH
Rows 1-4: Knit.
Row 5 (RS): K8, p1, k6, [p1, k1] 3 times, p1, k24.
Row 6 (WS): K2, p23, [k1, p1] twice, k1, p6, k1, p1, k1, p5, k2.
Row 7: K6, [p1, k1] twice, p1, k4, [p1, k1] 3 times, p1, k24.
Row 8: K2, p23, [k1, p1] twice, k1, p4, [k1, p1] 3 times, k1, p3, k2.
Row 9: K4, [p1, k1] 4 times, p1, k2, [p1, k1] 3 times, p1, k24.
Row 10: K2, p23, [k1, p1] twice, k1, p2, [k1, p1] 6 times, k2.
Row 11: Rep row 9.
Row 12: Rep row 8.
Row 13: Rep row 7.
Row 14: Rep row 6.
Row 15: Rep row 5.
Row 16: K2, p23, [k1, p1] twice, k1, p14, k2.
Rep rows 5-16 until block measures length specified in the Written Instructions on p57, ending with a WS row.
Next 4 rows: Knit.

BLOCK 3: FILEY
Rows 1-4: Knit.
Row 5 (RS): K8, p1, k6, p2, [k1, p1] 3 times, k1, p2, k20.
Row 6 (WS): K2, p18, k3, [p1, k1] twice, p1, k3, p5, k1, p1, k1, p5, k2.
Row 7: K6, p1, k3, p1, k4, p2, [k1, p1] 3 times, k1, p2, k20.
Row 8: K2, p18, k3, [p1, k1] twice, p1, k3, p3, k1, p5, k1, p3, k2.

Row 9: K4, p1, k7, p1, k2, p2, [k1, p1] 3 times, k1, p2, k20.
Row 10: K2, p18, k3, [p1, k1] twice, p1, k3, p1, k1, p9, k1, p1, k2.
Rep rows 5-10 until block measures length specified in the Written Instructions on p57, ending with a WS row.
Next 4 rows: Knit.

BLOCK 4: WHITBY
Rows 1-3: Knit.
Row 4 (WS): K13, m1p, k4, m1p, k29. *48 sts*
Row 5 (RS): K28, p1, k6, p1, k12.
Row 6: K2, p10, k1, p6, k1, p26, k2.
Row 7: K4, [p2, k2] 6 times, p1, k6, p1, [k2, p2] twice, k4.
Row 8: [K2, p2] 3 times, k1, p6, k1, [p2, k2] 7 times.
Row 9: K28, p1, C6B, p1, k12.
Row 10: Rep row 6.
Row 11: Rep row 7.
Row 12: Rep row 8.
Row 13: Rep row 5.
Row 14: Rep row 6.
Row 15: K4, [p2, k2] 6 times, p1, C6B, p1, [k2, p2] twice, k4.
Row 16: Rep row 8.
Rep rows 5-16 until block measures length specified in the Written Instructions on p57, ending with a WS row.
Next row: K29, k2tog, k4, k2tog, k13. *46 sts*
Next 3 rows: Knit.

BLOCK 5: ROBIN HOOD'S BAY
Rows 1-3: Knit.
Row 4 (WS): K10, m1p, k4, m1p, k32. *48 sts*
Row 5 (RS): K3, [p1, k1] 14 times, p1, k6, p2, [k1, p1] 3 times, k2.
Row 6: K3, [p1, k1] twice, p1, k2, p6, [k1, p1] 15 times, k2.
Row 7: K2, [p1, k1] 14 times, p2, k6, [p1, k1] 3 times, p1, k3.
Row 8: K2, [p1, k1] 4 times, p6, k2, [p1, k1] 13 times, p1, k3.
Row 9: K3, [p1, k1] 14 times, p1, C6B, p2, [k1, p1] 3 times, k2.
Row 10: Rep row 6.
Row 11: Rep row 7.
Row 12: Rep row 8.
Row 13: As row 5.
Row 14: Rep row 6.
Row 15: K2, [p1, k1] 14 times, p2, C6B, [p1, k1] 3 times, p1, k3.
Row 16: Rep row 8.
Rep rows 5-16 until block measures length specified in the Written Instructions on p57, ending with a WS row.
Next row: K29, k2tog, k4, k2tog, k13. *46 sts*
Next 3 rows: Knit.

WRITTEN INSTRUCTIONS

STRIPS 1 AND 3
Using 4mm ndls, cast on 46 sts.

Using colour and stitch pattern shown in the Assembly Diagram, work in stitch pattern reading from the Chart or Written Instructions. Rep patt as specified until piece measures 43cm/17" from cast-on edge, then work last 4 rows. Break yarn.

Using next colour and stitch pattern given in Assembly Diagram, work in stitch pattern given reading from the Chart or Written Instructions. Rep patt as specified until piece measures 43cm/17" from change of colour, then work last 4 rows. Break yarn.

Using next colour and stitch pattern shown in the Assembly Diagram, work in stitch pattern given reading from the Chart or Written Instructions. Rep patt as specified until piece measures 43cm/17" from change of colour, then work last 4 rows. Cast off.

STRIPS 2 AND 4
Cast on 46 sts. Using colour and stitch pattern shown in the Assembly Diagram, work in stitch pattern reading from the Chart or Written Instructions. Rep patt as specified until piece measures 21cm/8¼" from cast-on edge, then work last 4 rows.

Break yarn.

Using next colour and stitch pattern given in the Assembly Diagram, work in stitch pattern reading from the Chart or Written Instructions. Rep patt as specified until piece measures 43cm/17" from change of colour, then work last 4 rows. Break yarn.

Using next colour and stitch pattern given in the Assembly Diagram, work in stitch pattern reading from the Chart or Written Instructions. Rep patt as specified until piece measures 43cm/17" from change of colour, then work last 4 rows. Break yarn.

Using next colour and stitch pattern given in the Assembly Diagram, work in stitch pattern reading from the Chart or Written Instructions. Rep patt as specified until piece measures 21cm/8¼" from change of colour, then work last 4 rows. Cast off.

FINISHING
Block all strips to measurements.
Sew together the four strips as shown in Assembly Diagram. We suggest using the 'mattress stitch for garter' method of seaming – a tutorial can be found at http://www.simple-knitting.com/seaming-garter-stitch.html

Charts appear on following pages.

CHARTS

KEY

☐ RS: knit WS: purl

• RS: purl WS: knit

▨ no stitch

⟆ m1p

╱ k2tog

⟆⟆ C6B

☐ repeat

CHART 1: WITHERNSEA

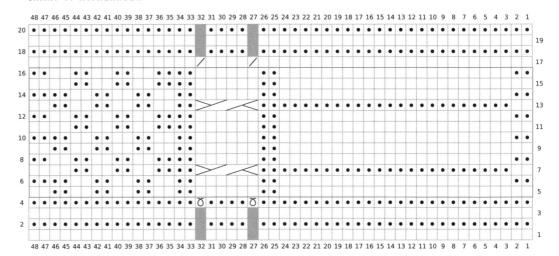

CHART 2: FLAMBOROUGH

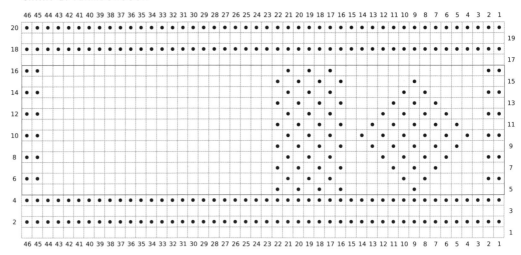

CHART 3: FILEY

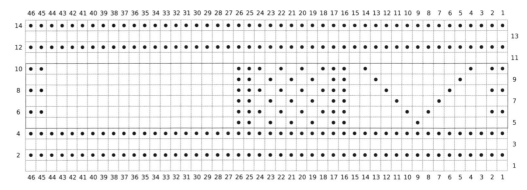

CHART 4: WHITBY

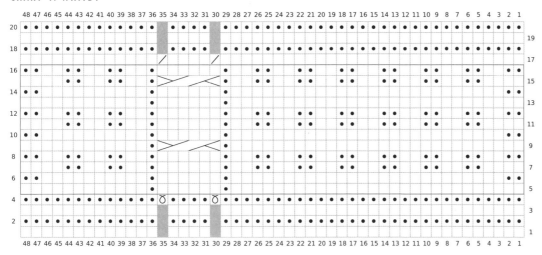

CHART 5: ROBIN HOOD'S BAY

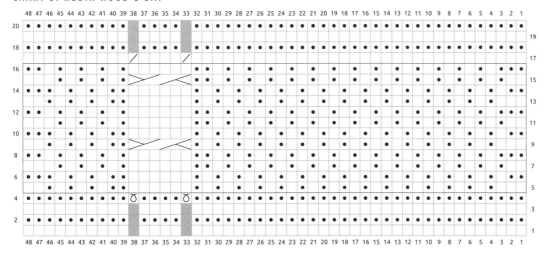

ASSEMBLY DIAGRAM

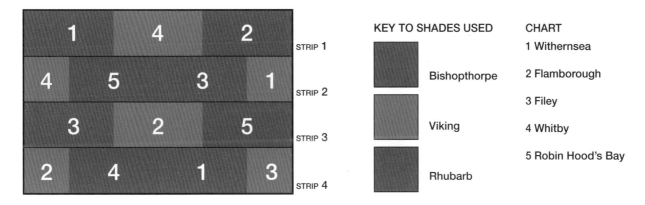

KEY TO SHADES USED	CHART
Bishopthorpe	1 Withernsea
Viking	2 Flamborough
Rhubarb	3 Filey
	4 Whitby
	5 Robin Hood's Bay

whitby

by Alison Moreton

Inspired by "Whitby Pattern IV" from *Patterns for Guernseys, Jerseys and Arans*: The traditional Betty Martin stitch pattern becomes a stretchy fabric that, when worked on small needles, is perfect for socks.

PATTERN NOTES

The cable has been modified to cross every 8th row to fit with the 4 row repeat of Betty Martin. For an even more authentic version, cross the cable every 7th row as in the original pattern.

YARN USED

baa ram ewe Dovestone DK, shown in shades:
Endeavour, 1 (2) x 100g skein(s)
Goathland, 1 (2) x 100g skein(s)

GAUGE

28 sts x 38 rows = 10cm/4" blocked and measured over stocking stitch on 3mm (US 2.5) needles

NEEDLES USED

3mm (US 2.5) DPNs

OTHER SUPPLIES

Stitch markers
Cable needle

SIZING

Sizes: S/M (M/L)
To fit foot circumference up to 21.5 (25.5)cm/8½ (10)"
See notes on sizing overleaf

CHARTS: WRITTEN INSTRUCTIONS

RIGHT CABLE PANEL

WORKED OVER 10 STS AND 8 RNDS
Rnds 1-3: P2, k6, p2.
Rnd 4: P2, C6B, p2.
Rnds 5-8: P2, k6, p2.

LEFT CABLE PANEL

WORKED OVER 10 STS AND 8 RNDS
Rnds 1-3: P2, k6, p2.
Rnd 4: P2, C6F, p2.
Rnds 5-8: P2, k6, p2.

SPECIAL INSTRUCTIONS

CABLES
C6B: Slip 3 sts to cn and hold in back, k3, k3 from cn
C6F: Slip 3 sts to cn and hold in front, k3, k3 from cn

ABBREVIATIONS

A list of standard abbreviations appears on page 72 and also on both cover flaps.

HINTS AND TIPS

CAST ON

It is important that the cast-on is nice and stretchy to make your socks easy to put on. Use a method such as the long-tail cast on and if you tend to work quite tightly, try casting on over a needle several sizes larger or two working needles held together.

SIZING AND YARN REQUIREMENTS

The pattern used is very stretchy which allows for some flexibility in sizing.

Size S/M is recommended for foot circumferences 16.5-20.5cm/6½-8" or children's shoe sizes UK 1-5/US 2-6/EU 33-38, and women's shoe sizes up to UK 6/US 8/ EU 39.
We used one 100g skein to make the S/M pair (shown in Goathland) to fit UK size 5 with only a small amount of yarn left over.

Size M/L is recommended for foot circumferences 19-24cm/7½-9½" or women's shoe sizes from UK 7/US 9/ EU 40 and all men's sizes.
We needed two 100g skeins to make the M/L pair shown in Endeavour to fit UK size 9 and used approximately 10g of the second skein.

FOOT LENGTHS

If you are unable to measure the wearer's feet, suggested foot lengths are given below:

UK shoe size	US shoe size	EU shoe size	Total foot length	
			cm	in
1-3	Child 2-4 Women 3-5	33-36	20.5	8
3-5	Child 4-6 Women 5-7	36-38	21.5	8½
5-7	Women 7-9 Men 6-8	38-40	23	9
7-9	Women 9-11 Men 8-10	40-42	25.5	10
9-11	Men 10-12	42-45	28	11

KEY

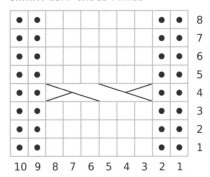

☐ knit

▣ purl

C6F

C6B

CHART: LEFT CABLE PANEL

CHART: RIGHT CABLE PANEL

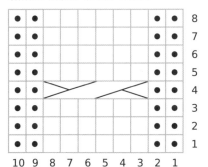

WRITTEN INSTRUCTIONS

RIGHT SOCK

CUFF

Using a stretchy method (see Hints and Tips), cast on 48 (56) sts. Join to work in the rnd, being careful not to twist and pm to indicate beg of rnd.

Rnd 1: Reading from the Chart or Written Instructions, work Right Cable Panel over next 10 sts, pm, k2, *p2, k2; rep from * to end.
Rnds 2-8: Work next row of Right Cable Panel over next 10 sts, sm, k2, *p2, k2; rep from * to end.
Note: Continue working reps of Right Cable Panel where indicated throughout.

LEG

Rnds 1-2: Work Right Cable Panel over next 10 sts, sm, k to end.
Rnds 3-4: Work Right Cable Panel over next 10 sts, sm, k2, *p2, k2; rep from * to end.
Rep rnds 1-4 working reps of the Right Cable Panel until sock measures 18cm/7" from cast-on edge.

**HEEL FLAP

Set-up row: Turn work so WS is facing. P24 (28) sts. Heel flap will be worked over these 24 (28) sts only – leave rem sts on hold for instep and remove beg of rnd m.

Working back and forth in rows, continue as foll:
Row 1 (RS): *Sl1 pwise wyib, k1; rep from * to end.
Row 2 (WS): Sl1 pwise wyif, p to end.
Rep rows 1-2 a further 11 (13) times.

HEEL TURN
Work as foll for your size decreasing one st every row:

SIZE S/M ONLY
Row 1 (RS): K14, ssk, k1, turn.
Row 2 (WS): Sl1, p5, p2tog, p1, turn.
Row 3: Sl1, k6, ssk, k1, turn.
Row 4: Sl1, p7, p2tog, p1, turn.
Row 5: Sl1, k8, ssk, k1, turn.
Row 6: Sl1, p9, p2tog, p1, turn.
Row 7: Sl1, k10, ssk, k1, turn.
Row 8: Sl1, p11, p2tog, p1, turn.
Row 9: Sl1, k12, ssk, turn without working the next st.
Row 10: Sl1, p12, p2tog, turn without working the next st. *14 heel sts rem*

SIZE M/L ONLY

Row 1 (RS): K16, ssk, k1, turn.
Rows 2-8: As size S/M.
Row 9: Sl1, k12, ssk, k1, turn.
Row 10: Sl1, p13, p2tog, p1, turn.
Row 11: Sl1, k14, ssk, turn without working the next st.
Row 12: Sl1, p14, p2tog, turn without working the next st. *16 heel sts rem*

GUSSET

Set-up rnd: K14 (16) heel sts, pick up and k12 (14) sts along heel flap edge, pick up and k1 st in corner between heel flap and instep, pm, work across 24 (28) instep sts in patt as set, pm, pick up and k1 st from corner between heel flap and instep, pick up and k12 (14) sts along edge of heel flap, k7 (8), pm for new beg of rnd at centre of sole. *64 (72) sts*

Rnd 1: K to 3 sts before m, k2tog, k1, sm, patt across instep sts, sm, k1, ssk, k to end.
Rnd 2: K to m, sm, patt across instep sts, sm, k to end.
Rep rnds 1-2 until 48 (56) sts remain.

FOOT

Next rnd: K to marker, sm, patt across instep sts as set, sm, k to end.
Rep last rnd until foot measures 4 (4.5cm)/1½ (1¾)" less than desired length, from back of heel flap and ending after completing rnd 8 of cable patt.

TOE

Knit 2 rnds.

Shape toe as foll:
Rnd 1: K9 (11), k2tog, k1, sm, k1, ssk, k18 (22), k2tog, k1, sm, k1, ssk, k to end. *44 (52) sts*
Rnd 2: Knit.
Rnd 3: [K to 3 sts before m, k2tog, k1, sm, k1, ssk] twice, k to end. *2 sts dec*
Rnd 4: Knit.
Rep rnds 3-4 a further 3 (4) times, then rep rnd 3 only once more. *20 (28) sts*

K to first m and stop.
Break yarn and graft toe closed using Kitchener stitch.

FINISHING

Weave in ends and block.

LEFT SOCK

CUFF

Cast on 48 (56) sts. Join to work in the rnd, being careful not to twist and pm to indicate beg of rnd.

Rnd 1: K2, [p2, k2] 3 (4) times, pm, reading from the Chart or Written Instructions, work Left Cable Panel over next 10 sts, pm, *k2, p2; rep from * to end.
Rnds 2-8: K2, [p2, k2] 3 (4) times, sm, work next row of Left Cable Panel over next 10 sts, sm, *k2, p2; rep from * to end.
Note: Continue working reps of Left Cable Panel where indicated throughout.

LEG

Rnds 1-2: K to m, sm, work Left Cable Panel over next 10 sts, sm, k to end.
Rnds 3-4: K2, [p2, k2] 3 (4) times, sm, work Left Cable Panel over next 10 sts, sm, *k2, p2; rep from * to end.
Rep rnds 1-4, working reps of the Left Cable Panel until sock measures 18cm/7" from cast-on edge.

Rep rnds 1-4 until sock measures 18cm/7" from cast-on edge.

Continuing to work the Left Cable Panel, work instructions as for Right Sock from ** to end.

the ropes

by Graeme Knowles-Miller

Inspired by the strong ropes used aboard fishing vessels out in the North Sea, this fitted ladies' jumper plays on the alternative names for cable stitch, 'Links of love'. It was commonly the fisher-men's wives who would knit ganseys, taking huge amounts of love and care to finish – keeping their man comfortable and protected at sea. The welt plays with different widths of cable combined with rib to be visually interesting but practical, like the ganseys of old.

YARN USED
baa ram ewe Dovestone DK in shade:
Bantam, 4 (4, 5, 5, 6) x 100g skeins

GAUGE
22 sts x 30 rows = 10cm/4" blocked and measured over stocking stitch on 4mm (US 6) needles

NEEDLES USED
3.5mm (US 4) circular needle, 40cm/16" length
3.5mm (US 4) circular needle, 80cm/32" length
4mm (US 6) circular needle, 80cm/32" length
3.5mm (US 4) DPNs for sleeves
4mm (US 6) DPNs for sleeves

OTHER SUPPLIES
14 stitch markers
Stitch holders or scrap yarn
Cable needle

SPECIAL INSTRUCTIONS
CABLES
C2B: Sl 1 st to cn, hold in back, k1, k1 from cn.
C4B: Sl 2 sts to cn, hold in back, k2, k2 from cn.
C6B: Sl 3 sts to cn, hold in back, k3, k3 from cn.

SIZING
See sizing table on next page.

ABBREVIATIONS
A list of standard abbreviations appears on page 72 and also on both cover flaps.

HINTS AND TIPS
WRAP & TURN (W&T)
After a knit stitch:
Bring the yarn to the front between the needles. Slip the next stitch purlwise. Take the yarn to the back between the needles. Slip stitch back to left needle. Turn.
After a purl stitch:
Bring the yarn to the back between the needles. Slip the next stitch purlwise. Take the yarn to the front between the needles. Slip stitch back to right needle. Turn.
To pick up a wrap on a knit stitch:
Use right needle to pick up the wrap from the front to the back, then put needle into the stitch knitwise, knit wrap and stitch together.
To pick up a wrap on a purl stitch:
Use the right needle to pick up the wrap from the back to the front and place it on the left needle. Purl the wrap and the stitch together.

SIZING TABLE

	xs	s	m	l	xl	
TO FIT BUST						
	71-76	81-86	91.5-96.5	101.5-106.5	111.5-117	cm
	28-30	32-34	36-38	40-42	44-46	in
ACTUAL BUST – A ON SCHEMATIC						
	70	75	90	100.5	110.5	cm
	27½	29½	35½	39½	43½	in
HIPS – B ON SCHEMATIC						
	85	90	99	109	119.5	cm
	33½	35½	39	43	47	in
UNDERARM TO BOTTOM EDGE – C ON SCHEMATIC						
	39	40.5	40.5	40.5	42	cm
	15½	16	16	16	16½	in
NECK – D ON SCHEMATIC						
	49.5	51	52	53.5	54.5	cm
	19½	20	20½	21	21½	in
UPPER ARM – E ON SCHEMATIC						
	25	26	28	30.5	34.5	cm
	9¾	10¼	11	12	13½	in
SLEEVE LENGTH – F ON SCHEMATIC						
	44.5	45.5	46	47	47	cm
	17½	18	18	18½	18½	in

RAGLAN CABLE CHART

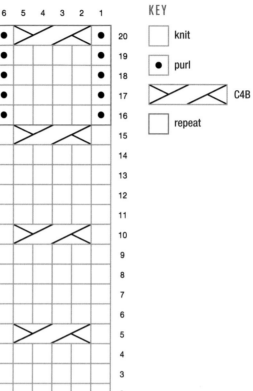

KEY

☐	knit
●	purl
⧅	C4B
☐	repeat

SCHEMATIC

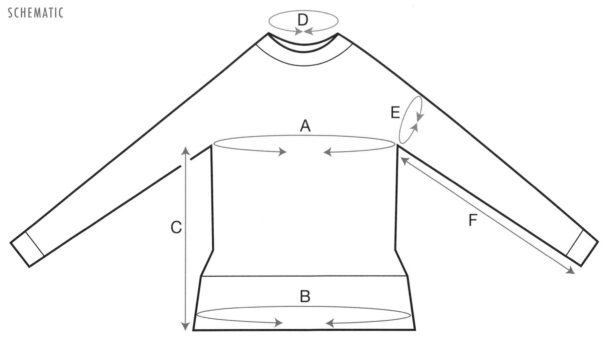

WRITTEN INSTRUCTIONS

BODY

Using 4mm ndl, cast on 240 (248, 268, 292, 312) sts. Join to work in the rnd, being careful not to twist and pm to indicate beg of rnd.

NOTE: Some knit sts are worked through the back loop (k tbl) – keep an eye out for these where separated by brackets, eg. k0 (0, 0, 0, 1) tbl to ensure you work them correctly.

Rnd 1: *P1, k4, p1, k0 (0, 0, 0, 1) tbl, p0 (0, 0, 0, 1), k0 (0, 0, 0, 1) tbl, p0 (0, 0, 0, 2), k0 (0, 0, 2, 2), p0 (0, 0, 2, 2), k0 (0, 0, 2, 2), p0 (0, 2, 2, 2), k0 (0, 3, 3, 3), p0 (2, 2, 2, 2), k2, p2, [k1 tbl, p1] twice, k1 tbl, p2, k2, p2, k3, p2, k2, p2, pm, k4, pm, p2, k2, p2, [k1 tbl, p1] twice, k1 tbl, p2, k2, p2, k3, p2, k2, p2, pm, k6, pm, p2, k2, p2, k3, p2, k2, p2, [k1 tbl, p1] twice, k1 tbl, p2, k2, p2, pm, k4, pm, p2, k2, p2, k3, p2, k2, p2, [k1 tbl, p1] twice, k1 tbl, p2, k2, p0 (2, 2, 2, 2), k0 (0, 3, 3, 3), p0 (0, 2, 2, 2), k0 (0, 0, 2, 2), p0 (0, 0, 2, 2), k0 (0, 0, 2, 2), p0 (0, 0, 0, 2), k0 (0, 0, 0, 1) tbl, p0 (0, 0, 0, 1), k0 (0, 0, 0, 1) tbl, pm; rep from * once more. *14 markers placed*

Rnd 2: *P1, k4, p1, k0 (0, 0, 0, 1) tbl, p0 (0, 0, 0, 1), k0 (0, 0, 0, 1) tbl, p0 (0, 0, 0, 2), k0 (0, 0, 2, 2), p0 (0, 0, 2, 2), [C2B] (0, 0, 1, 1) time, p0 (0, 2, 2, 2), k0 (0, 3, 3, 3), p0 (2, 2, 2, 2), C2B, p2, [k1 tbl, p1] twice, k1 tbl, p2, C2B, p2, k3, p2, C2B, p2, sm, k4, sm, p2, C2B, p2, [k1 tbl, p1] twice, k1 tbl, p2, C2B, p2, k3, p2, C2B, p2, sm, k6, sm, p2, C2B, p2, k3, p2, C2B, p2, [k1 tbl, p1] twice, k1 tbl, p2, C2B, p2, sm, k4, sm, p2, C2B, p2, k3, p2, C2B, p2, [k1 tbl, p1] twice, k1 tbl, p2, C2B, p0 (2, 2, 2, 2), k0 (0, 3, 3, 3), p0 (0, 2, 2, 2), [C2B] 0 (0, 0, 1, 1) time, p0 (0, 0, 2, 2), k0 (0, 0, 2, 2) times, p0 (0, 0, 0, 2), k0 (0, 0, 0, 1) tbl, p0 (0, 0, 0, 1), k0 (0, 0, 0, 1) tbl, sm; rep from * once more.

Rnd 3: *P1, k4, p1, patt to m, sm, k4, sm, patt to m, sm, k6, sm, patt to m, sm, k4, sm, patt to m, sm; rep from * once more.

Rnd 4: Rep rnd 2.

Rnd 5: *P1, C4B, p1, patt to m, sm, C4B, sm, patt to m, sm, k6, sm, patt to m, sm, C4B, sm, patt to m, sm; rep from * once more.

Rnd 6: Rep rnd 2.

Rnd 7: *Patt to m, sm, k4, sm, patt to m, sm, C6B, sm, patt to m, sm, k4, sm, patt to m, sm; rep from * once more.

Rnd 8: Rep rnd 2.
Rnd 9: Rep rnd 3.
Rnd 10: Rep rnd 5.
Rnd 11: Rep rnd 3.

Rnd 12: Rep rnd 2.
Rnd 13: Rep rnd 3.
Rnd 14: Rep rnd 7.
Rnd 15: Rep rnd 5.
Rnd 16-19: Rep rnds 2-3.

Rnd 20: *P1, C4B, p1, k0 (0, 0, 0, 1) tbl, p0 (0, 0, 0, 1), k0 (0, 0, 0, 1) tbl, p0 (0, 0, 0, 2), k0 (0, 0, 2, 2), p0 (0, 0, 2, 2), [k2tog] 0 (0, 0, 1, 1) time, p0 (0, 2, 2, 2), k0 (0, 3, 3, 3), p0 (2, 2, 2, 2), k2tog, p2, [k1 tbl, p1] twice, k1 tbl, p2, k2tog, p2, k3, p2, k2tog, p2, sm, C4B, sm, p2, k2tog, p2, [k1 tbl, p1] twice, k1 tbl, p2, k2tog, p2, k3, p2, k2tog, p2, sm, k6, sm, p2, k2tog, p2, k3, p2, k2tog, p2, [k1 tbl, p1] twice, k1 tbl, p2, k2tog, p2, sm, C4B, sm, p2, k2tog, p2, k3, p2, k2tog, p2, [k1 tbl, p1] twice, k1 tbl, p2, k2tog, p0 (2, 2, 2, 2), k0 (0, 3, 3, 3), p0 (0, 2, 2, 2), [k2tog] 0 (0, 0, 1, 1) time, p0 (0, 0, 2, 2), k0 (0, 0, 2, 2), p0 (0, 0, 0, 2), k0 (0, 0, 0, 1) tbl, p0 (0, 0, 0, 1), k0 (0, 0, 0, 1) tbl, sm; rep from * once more. *216 (224, 244, 264, 284) sts*

Rnd 21: Rep rnd 7.
Rnd 22: *Patt as set to m, sm; rep from * to end.

Rnd 23: *P1, C4B, p1, k0 (0, 0, 0, 1) tbl, p0 (0, 0, 0, 1), k0 (0, 0, 0, 1) tbl, p0 (0, 0, 0, 2), k0 (0, 0, 2, 2), p0 (0, 0, 2, 2), k0 (0, 0, 1, 1), p0 (0, 2, 2, 2), [k2tog] 0 (0, 1, 1, 1) time, k0 (0, 1, 1, 1), p0 (2, 2, 2, 2), k1, p2, [k1 tbl, p1] twice, k1 tbl, p2, k1, p2, k2tog, k1, p2, k1, p2, sm, k4, sm, p2, k1, p2, [k1 tbl, p1] twice, k1 tbl, p2, k1, p2, k2tog, k1, p2, k1, p2, sm, k6, sm, p2, k1, p2, k2tog, k1, p2, k1, p2, [k1 tbl, p1] twice, k1 tbl, p2, k1, p2, sm, k4, sm, p2, k1, p2, k2tog, k1, p2, k1, p2, [k1 tbl, p1] twice, k1 tbl, p2, k1, p0 (2, 2, 2, 2), k2tog 0 (0, 1, 1, 1), k0 (0, 1, 1, 1), p0 (0, 2, 2, 2), k0 (0, 0, 1, 1), p0 (0, 0, 2, 2), k0 (0, 0, 2, 2), p0 (0, 0, 0 , 2), k0 (0, 0, 0, 1) tbl, p0 (0, 0, 0, 1), k0 (0, 0, 0, 1) tbl, sm; rep from * once more. *208 (216, 232, 252, 272) sts*

Rnd 24: Rep rnd 22.
Rnd 25: Rep rnd 5.

Rnd 26: *P1, k4, p1, k0 (0, 0, 0, 1) tbl, p0 (0, 0, 0, 1), k0 (0, 0, 0, 1) tbl, p0 (0, 0, 0, 2), k0 (0, 0, 2, 2), p0 (0, 0, 2, 2), k0 (0, 0, 1, 1), p0 (0, 2, 2, 2), k0 (0, 2, 2, 2), p0 (2, 2, 2, 2), k1, p2, [k1 tbl, p1] twice, k1 tbl, p2, k1, p2tog, k2, p2, k1, p2, sm, k4, sm, p2, k1, p2, [k1 tbl, p1] twice, k1 tbl, p2, k1, p2tog, k2, p2tog, k1, p2, sm, k6, sm, p2, k1, p2tog, k2, p2tog, k1, p2, [k1 tbl, p1] twice, k1 tbl, p2, k1, p2, sm, k4, sm, p2, k1, p2, k2, p2tog, k1, p2, [k1 tbl, p1] twice, k1 tbl, p2, k1, p0 (2, 2, 2, 2), [k2tog] 0 (0, 1, 1, 1) time, k0 (0, 1, 1, 1), p0 (0, 2, 2, 2), k0 (0, 0, 1, 1), p0 (0, 0, 2, 2), k0 (0, 0, 2, 2), p0 (0, 0, 2, 2), k0 (0, 0, 0, 1) tbl, p0 (0, 0, 0, 1), k0 (0, 0, 0, 1) tbl, sm; rep from * once more. *196 (204, 218, 238, 258) sts*

Rnd 27: Rep rnd 3.
Rnd 28: Rep rnd 7.

Rnd 29: *P1, k4, p1, k0 (0, 0, 0, 1) tbl, p0 (0, 0, 0, 1), k0 (0, 0, 0, 1) tbl, [p2tog] 0 (0, 0, 0, 1) time, k0 (0, 0, 2, 2), [p2tog] 0 (0, 0, 1, 1) time, k0 (0, 0, 1, 1), p0 (0, 2, 2, 2), k0 (0, 2, 2, 2), [p2tog] 0 (1, 1, 1, 1) time, k1, p2, [k1 tbl, p1] twice, k1 tbl, p2, k1, p1, k2tog, p2, k1, p2, sm, k4, sm, p2, k1, p2tog, [k1 tbl, p1] twice, k1 tbl, p2, k1, p1, k2, p1, k1, p2, sm, k6, sm, p2, k1, p1, k2, p1, k1, p2, [k1 tbl, p1] twice, p2tog, k1, p2, sm, k4, sm, p2, k1, p2, k2tog, p1, k1, p2tog, [k1 tbl, p1] twice, k1 tbl, p2, k1, [p2tog] 0 (1, 1, 1, 1) time, k0 (0, 2, 2, 2), p0 (0, 2, 2, 2), k0 (0, 0, 1, 1), [p2tog] 0 (0, 0, 1, 1) time, k0 (0, 0, 2, 2), [p2tog] 0 (0, 0, 0, 1) time, k0 (0, 0, 0, 1) tbl, p0 (0, 0, 0, 1), k0 (0, 0, 0, 1) tbl, sm; rep from * once more. *184 (188, 202, 218, 234) sts*

Rnd 30: Rep rnd 5.
Rnd 31: *P1, k4, p1, patt to m, sm, k2tog, k2, sm, patt to m, sm, k6, sm, patt to m, sm, k2tog, k2, sm, patt to m, sm; rep from * once more. *180 (184, 198, 214, 230) sts*

Rnd 32: Rep rnd 22.

Rnd 33: *P1, k4, p1, k4 (5, 9, 13, 17), k2tog, k6, k2tog, k3, rm, k1, k2tog, rm, k8, k2tog, k2, k2tog, k3, p2, sm, k6, sm, k4, k2tog, k2, k2tog, k7, rm, k1, k2tog, rm, k3, k2tog, k6, k2tog, k5 (6, 10, 14, 18), sm; rep from * once more. *160 (164, 178, 194, 210) sts*

Rnd 34: *P1, k4, p1, k to 2 sts before m, p2tog, rm, k6, rm, p2tog, k to m, sm; rep from * once more. *156 (160, 174, 190, 206) sts*

Rnd 35: *P1, C4B, p1, k to m, sm; rep from * once more.

Dec rnd: *P1, k4, p1, k2tog, k21 (21, 24, 28, 29), [k2tog] 1 (1, 1, 1, 0) time, k0 (0, 0, 0, 2), pm, k22 (24, 26, 29, 32), pm, k0 (0, 0, 0, 2), [ssk] 1 (1, 1, 1, 0) time, k to 2 sts before m, ssk, sm; rep from * once more. New markers indicate points of decrease for shaping. *8 (8, 8, 8, 4) sts dec. 148 (152, 166, 182, 202) sts*

Work 2 rnds straight in patt slipping markers as you come to them.

Rep last 3 rnds a further 3 (2, 1, 0, 0) times. *124 (136, 158, -, -) sts*

Work 2 (4, 2, 10, 9) rounds in patt as set.
Work 1 rnd in patt decreasing - (-, 2, 6, 2) sts evenly. *124 (136, 156, 178, 200) sts*

WAIST

Inc rnd: *P1, k4, p1, sm, m1l, k to m, m1r, sm; rep from * once more. *4 sts inc. 128 (140, 160, 180, 204) sts*
Continue in patt and rep Inc rnd every 12 (11, 7, 6, 7) rnds a further 6 (7, 10, 11, 10) times continuing to work cables as set every 5 rnds. *152 (168, 200, 224, 244) sts*

If necessary, work straight in St st with cable twists as set until piece measures 39.5 (40.5, 40.5, 40.5, 40.5, 42)cm/15½ (16, 16, 16, 16, 16½)" from cast-on edge. Place all sts on a st holder.

SLEEVES

MAKE 2 ALIKE
Using 3.5mm DPNs cast on 42 (42, 44, 46, 50) sts. Join to work in the rnd, being careful not to twist and pm to indicate beg of rnd.

Rib rnd: *K1, p1; rep from * to end.
Rep Rib rnd until cuff measures 5cm/2".

Change to 4mm DPNs.
Work St st in the rnd (knit every rnd) for 17 (13, 12, 10, 8) rnds.
Inc rnd: K1, m1l, k to last st, m1r, k1. *2 sts inc; 44 (44, 46, 48, 52) sts*
Continue in St st and rep Inc rnd every 18 (14, 13, 11, 9) rnds a further 5 (7, 8, 9, 12) times. *54 (58, 62, 66, 76) sts*

Work straight until sleeve measures 44.5 (45.5, 46, 47, 47) cm/17½ (18, 18, 18½, 18½)" from cast-on edge.
K3 (4, 4, 5, 5) and place these plus the last 3 (4, 4, 5, 5) sts of previous rnd on a stitch holder and rem 48 (50, 54, 56, 66) sts on a separate holder.

RAGLAN

Set-up for raglan: With RS facing, working across the body sts, k3 (4, 4, 5, 5) sts (this gets the working yarn to right place for beg of next rnd), and place these 3 (4, 4, 5, 5) sts, plus last 3 (4, 4, 5, 5) sts of previous rnd, on a stitch holder. Without knitting the sts, slipping them from left-hand to right-hand ndl, continue as foll:
Sl 6 sts, pm, sl 58 (64, 80, 90, 100) sts, pm, sl 6 sts, pm, place next 6 (8, 8, 10, 10) sts from body on a stitch holder, sl all sts from first sleeve to right-hand ndl, pm, sl 6 sts, pm, sl 58 (64, 80, 90, 100) sts, pm, sl 6 sts, pm, sl all sts from second sleeve to right-hand ndl, pm for new beg of rnd. *8 markers placed; 236 (252, 292, 316, 356) sts*

Work raglan shaping as foll:
Note: Beg on the next rnd, work Raglan Cable Chart across each of the four 6 st sections between raglan markers working rows 1-20 once and then work reps of rows 16-20 only for remainder of raglan section.

K 2 rnds working the four sets of 6 raglan sts in cable patt.

Dec rnd: *K6, sm, ssk, k to 2 sts before next m, k2tog sm; rep from * a further 3 times. *8 sts dec; 228 (244, 284, 308, 348) sts*
Continue in St st and cable patt as set and rep Dec rnd every 3 rnds a further 12 (9, 19, 24, 13) times, then every 7 (4, 5, -, 2) rnds 2 (7, 2, -, 16) times. *116 (116, 116, 116, 116) sts*

Work 1 (-, 1, -, 1) rnd straight.

Shape the shoulders with short rows as foll:
Short row 1 (RS): Patt 12 sts, w&t,
Short row 2 (WS): Patt to 6 sts after right neck marker (third m when counted with RS facing), w&t.
Short row 3: Patt to 2 sts before wrapped st, w&t.
Short row 4: Patt to 2 sts before wrapped st, w&t.
Rep short rows 3-4 once more until 2 sts remain at each neck side of cable.

Next short row (RS): Knit to end of rnd.
Patt 1 rnd picking up and working the wraps with their st as you pass them.

NECKBAND
Change to 3.5mm ndls.
Rnd 1: *K1, p1; rep from * to end.
Rib rnd: *K1, p1; rep from * to end
Rep Rib rnd until collar measures 2.5cm/1".
Cast off in loosely in rib.

FINISHING
Graft underarms sts using Kitchener stitch.
Weave in ends and block to measurements.

ACKNOWLEDGMENTS

We would like to thank all the amazing people who made this book happen:

Joelle Trousdale, for her project co-ordination and superb photography in the beautiful Yorkshire coastal village of Staithes.

Rachel Atkinson for excellent tech editing in the face of adversity!

Nic Blackmore for turning all the components into a beautiful book.

Katherine Johnson, Claire Pascoe and Millie Holmes, our fabulous models, for enduring cold and windy weather to make everything look lovely.

Our super sample knitters who turned our ideas into reality: **Sarah Holmes, Katherine Johnson, Sam Kain, Tina McAra, Sue Fenton, Sue Cauldwell, Dawn Beck**.

The Cod & Lobster and Dotty's Tearooms in Staithes for providing excellent food and drink and even a mug to model the mitts!

Flora Cox for her inspiring love of the coast.

And of course **Verity, Jo** and the whole team at **baa ram ewe** for their support in making this book possible.

BIBLIOGRAPHY

Doherty, Elizabeth (2015). *Top Down: Reimagining Set-In Sleeve Design*. Maine: Quince & Co.

Hemingway, Penelope Lister (2015) *River Ganseys: Strikin' t'loop, Swaving, and Other Yorkshire Knitting Curiosities Revived from the Archives*. Lakewood: Cooperative Press.

Logan, Kathryn (2013). *Fishing for Ganseys*. Edinburgh: Allander: Moray Firth Partnership.

Thompson, Gladys (1971). *Patterns for Guernseys, Jerseys & Arans: Fishermen's Sweaters from the British Isles*. Mineola, New York: Dover Publications.

C.D. Moorby (2012) *More Gansey: Für Wind und Wetter* Available http://www.stitchedandstitched.com/?p=1685. Last accessed [Feb 2016]

Flamborough Marine (2001) *The Story Behind the Gansey* Available http://www.ganseys.co.uk/. Last accessed [Feb 2016]

Gansey nation (2015) *Ganseys* Available: http://www.ganseys.com/ganseys/ganseys-1/. Last accessed [Feb 2016]

Propagansey (2016) *Ganseys* Available http://www.propagansey.co.uk/. Last accessed [April 2016]